STARTING FROM SCRATCH

SHARON GLASS

CONTENTS

INTRODUCTION

One of my earliest childhood memories is of me standing in the kitchen of our home in Johannesburg. My father, who was in the building industry, had built our house himself and in it the kitchen was the centre of everything. It was wonderfully large and open with two built-in ovens, a large hob, seating area, lots of cupboards and a separate scullery. It was very posh (considering it was built in the 1960s) and always a hub of activity. At home, if ever we were looking for someone, we'd likely find him or her in the kitchen! And even today, things haven't changed much – my family usually finds me in the kitchen, around which everything seems to revolve. I have tried to share my love of cooking with my own children, inviting them to participate as much as possible.

When I was a child, my family's lives revolved around food, whether it was breakfast, lunch, dinner or a light snack. My mother loved cooking and I was like her shadow in the kitchen, sitting on the counter, observing how she did things and making notes of her recipes and methods.

When I cook today, I do it with abundance and pleasure and put my heart into the food. I always aim to arouse the senses with a balance of flavour, colour and texture and it gives me pleasure when I put a dish on the table and my family enjoys it. In keeping with the growing trend towards healthier living, I try to monitor the ingredients I use – cooking with olive and grape seed oils, buying organic where possible and growing my own herbs and some veggies.

Before you start cooking, there are some easy rules that you should follow and while they do sound rudimentary, they really will make trying out recipes so much easier!

Always remember to be organized, read the recipe, make sure you have all the ingredients, work in an orderly manner and clean up as you prepare... and most important, take pleasure in your cooking, taste your food as you go along and follow the basics. Remember that the process of cooking can be as nourishing and satisfying as the food itself.

PANTRY ESSENTIALS

Here are some basics both perishable and non-perishable which you should have in your kitchen and will give you the basis to cook anything at the drop of a hat.

PANTRY STAPLES

Olive oil	good quality extra virgin and light olive oil
Vinegar	red & white wine, balsamic, white spirit
Salt	sea salt
Black pepper	freshly ground
Spices	good variety
Dried herbs	always use fresh herbs where possible
Pasta	penne, fettuccine, fusilli, etc.
Rice	basmati, jasmine, Tastic, health
Tinned tomatoes	Italian whole and chopped
Capers	
Flours	cake flour, self-raising
Sugars	white, castor, icing, sticky brown
Baking powder	
Bicarbonate of soda	
Tinned fruit	pie apples, peaches, lychees
Vanilla essence	
Cocoa powder	
Yeast	dry instant yeast
Jam	apricot, strawberry
Wine	white, red
Stock powder	chicken, beef, vegetable
Tinned fish	tuna, salmon

PERISHABLES

Garlic	fresh cloves
Onions	red and white
Potatoes	Mediterranean and baking
Carrots	
Lemons	
Eggs	
Fresh herbs	lovely to grow your own in pots
Mustards	Dijon & wholegrain
Cheeses	cheddar, cream, cottage
Nuts	pecan, almonds
Butter	salted, unsalted
Milk	long life and fresh
Bread	
Frozen puff	pastry
Frozen vegetables	peas, corn
Olives	Calamata and green

SUGGESTED KITCHEN EQUIPMENT

I am always asked how to stock a kitchen if starting from scratch. Here are some suggestions for a new kitchen:

2	Baking trays – 1 large and 1 small
1	Baster
1	Box grater
2	Chopping boards
1	Colander – for pasta
1	Corkscrew
1	2-cup glass measuring cup
3	Different sized non-stick frying pans
1	Egg slicer
1	Food processor
1	Hand blender
5	Knives:
	2 paring, 1 slicing, 1 large chef's knife, 1 carving
1	Knife block
1	Loaf tin
1	Loose bottom quiche tin – 24cm (9 inch)
1	Large kitchen spoon
1	Large slotted kitchen spoon
1	Lettuce spinner
1	Long handled meat fork
1	Set stainless steel or silicone measuring cups
2	Sets measuring spoons
1	Metal lifter
1	Metal palette knife
1	Metal steamer
1	Metal tong
3	Stainless steel or glass mixing bowls

1	Mix master or electric hand beater
1	12-hole muffin tin
2	Sets oven gloves – good quality
2	Pastry brushes – one silicone
1	Pepper mill
1	Pizza tin (with holes)
1	Set of pots – small, medium, large
1	Ridged non stick grilling pan
2	Roasting pans – 1 large, 1 small
1	Rolling pin
1	Sharp kitchen scissors
1	Sharpening tool for knives
1	Silicone lifter (for eggs)
2	Soup ladles
2	Rubber spatulas
1	Spaghetti measure
2	Springform tins – 26cm (10 inch) and 24cm (9 inch)
2	Strainers – 1 large, 1 small
1	Tin opener
1	Timer
1	Toaster
1	Vegetable peeler
2	Whisks – small and medium
1	Wok
3	Wooden spoons
1	Zester/microplane

HERBS AND SPICES

Always try to use fresh rather than dried herbs. Remember to use double the amount of fresh to dry. For example 1 T fresh basil = 1 t dry basil

Sweet basil	Large flat light green leaf with a strong sweet smell. Used mostly in Italian dishes, pastas etc. and sometimes in salads. Grows in hot, dry conditions.
Oregano	More aromatic and stronger flavour than basil. Used mostly in Italian dishes.
Rosemary	Woody upright stems with thin pointed leaves. Used in poultry and lamb dishes. Also used in pasta and tomato based dishes. Available all year round.
Thyme	Tiny oval leaf. Mostly used with chicken and meat and also in some sauces. Very distinct taste. Available all year round.
Italian parsley	Flat leaf parsley with more flavour than regular parsley.
Parsley	Curly leaf. Mostly used for decoration and colour. No distinct taste.
Coriander	Looks like flat leaf parsley but has a much stronger taste and is used in many Thai and Mexican dishes – also known as Cilantro.
Tarragon	Narrow leaves have a warm peppery-bitter scent with a hint of anise. Mostly in dry form. Used mostly with chicken dishes. Has a very delicate flavour. Available in summer.
Sage	Of the mint family. Has a highly aromatic flavour and silvery leaves. Very strong flavour. Used mostly in stuffing and also in Italian sauces with browned butter over pasta. Available most of the year.
Mint	Herb mostly used for decorating fruit but can be used in lamb dishes and for sauces. Likes to grow in the sun.
Lemongrass	Looks like grass. Strong lemony flavour. Use only the inside of the stem and chop very fine. Used in Asian sauces for flavour and also in stock to give a light lemon flavour.
Rocket	Available in 2 shapes – Wild Rocket – much smaller leaves shaped like a dandelion; or Regular rocket – small, lobed leaves on a stem, quite peppery in taste. Also known as arugula, roquette. Used in salads and sauces.
Nutmeg	Nutmeg is the actual seed of the nutmeg evergreen tree that produces two spices, nutmeg and mace. Available as a nut to grate fresh or ground in a bottle. Used mostly in white and cheese sauces.
Paprika	A variety of sweet red pepper. Not spicy. Used mostly for decoration.
Saffron	Derived from the flower of the saffron crocus. Has red/orange strands. Often dried and used in cooking as a seasoning and colouring agent. It is native to south-west Asia, first cultivated in Greece. Contains carotene dye which colours the food yellow. It is the world's most expensive spice.

EGGS

Eggs are healthy for you and the recommended weekly intake according to dieticians and The Heart and Stroke Foundation SA is 3-4. Look for eggs that are enriched with Omega 3 for added health benefits. I like to use jumbo or extra large eggs for baking and cooking. There is an art to something as simple as boiling or frying an egg. A non-stick frying pan is essential as a little non-stick cooking spray is all you need to coat the pan. Serving eggs on a slightly warmed plate keeps them hot until they are eaten. Here are some basic recipes:

BOILED

Half fill a small pot with cold water. Use room temperature eggs to avoid them cracking.
Add a little salt or vinegar to the water, then add the egg and bring to a boil on high heat. When boiling, turn heat down to medium and boil for:

15 minutes – hard boiled
10-12 minutes – medium
6-7 minutes – soft boiled

Remove egg from the pot, crack shell and place in ice water immediately. This shrinks the inside vacuum so that the shell peels off easily.

FRIED

Always preheat the frying pan. Spray with non-stick cooking spray or melt a small blob (about 1 t) butter or margarine. Break egg gently into pan and fry until white is set, shaking pan to ensure it is not catching. Turn with a lifter and fry other side for another few minutes. Gently slide out of frying pan onto a plate. "Sunnyside eggs" are fried on one side only.

SCRAMBLED

Beat 2 eggs with a whisk. Add 2 T milk, salt and a drop of pepper.

Whisk well. Prepare a small frying pan with non-stick spray or with a little margarine or butter on medium heat.

Do not allow pan to get too hot as a scrambled eggs should not brown. Stir eggs all the time with a lifter whilst cooking, until almost set but not quite firm.

OMELETTE

Break 2 eggs into a small mixing bowl. Whisk with a little milk or water. Add salt and pepper.

Spray a pan with non-stick spray or melt a little butter into the pan on medium high heat. Pour egg mixture into the pan and gently lift the sides as they begin to set, allowing the uncooked egg to run under the sides and cook.

Grate some cheddar cheese and sprinkle on one side of the egg, allowing cheese to melt slightly. Then lift up and fold over half of egg. Brown for a few more minutes. Shake to loosen in pan and then slide out onto a plate.

SOUPS

Traditionally soups have been classified into two groups: clear broths and thick soups. The base of all soups is a stock of meat or chicken and vegetables (or just vegetables) which provides the foundation of body and flavour.

A rich and fragrant homemade stock will make a wonderful soup but if you are short of time use organic liquid stock available from shops. Powdered stock is convenient and easy to use and a generous amount is needed to give lots of flavour and body to a soup. Opt for varieties with no MSG.

Wherever stock powder is mentioned, mix with the specified quantity of boiling water.

BASIC CHICKEN SOUP

There is simply nothing nicer than a good old-fashioned chicken soup to warm the cockles of your heart (and to treat a cold it is widely believed). This recipe will become a staple in your family. Simply put it on the stove and forget about it (maybe look in the pot once or twice). It tastes better the longer it cooks.

1	whole chicken or 10 chicken pieces and 4 chicken backs
1	packet chicken giblets (about 250g)
6-8	carrots chunked
1	stick celery with the leaves
	few sprigs of parsley
1	onion, cut in 4
90ml (6 T)	chicken stock powder
2ℓ (8 cups)	cold water

PREPARATION TIME: 10 minutes
COOKING TIME: 3-4 hours

Place all ingredients in a large pot. Cover with the water and bring to the boil with the lid on. Turn down the heat and simmer with lid on for at least 3-4 hours. Add more water and stock if necessary.

Strain vegetables and chicken in a strainer. Liquidize only the carrots which will add a lovely colour in the liquid from the soup.

CHEF'S TIP: Always cool soup containing stock without the lid. This soup freezes very well. An old-fashioned custom is to use chicken feet for flavour but I find that the backs of the chicken and the giblets (not the liver) also give a great taste. A good quality stock powder is essential for a tasty soup. If you are not using stock powder, then simply add coarse salt or Herbamare at the end of the cooking.

Serves 8-10

COUNTRY MINESTRONE SOUP

Although this recipe may be daunting because of its length, it is so delicious that it's worth the effort. Sautéing the vegetables in the butter and oil will give them much more flavour than simply adding them to a pot full of water.

60ml (¼ cup)	olive oil
30ml (2 T)	butter or margarine
2	onions
3	large carrots
3	sticks celery
3	potatoes
4	zucchini
200g (7 oz)	green beans
¼	cabbage
½	butternut
225g (8 oz)	tin butter beans
2x410g (14 oz)	tins diced tomatoes
125ml (½ cup)	tomato purée
80ml (⅓ cup)	chicken or vegetable stock powder
3ℓ (12 cups)	boiling water
	coarse salt
	black pepper

PREPARATION TIME: 20 minutes
COOKING TIME: 3 hours

Prepare vegetables as follows: Coarsely chop onions, carrots, celery, potatoes and zucchini. Cut the green beans into small pieces, shred the cabbage and dice the butternut.

Heat the oil and butter in a large pot. Sauté onions, carrots, celery, potatoes and zucchini over medium heat until vegetables are golden brown. Add the rest of the prepared vegetables and the butter beans, tomatoes, tomato purée, stock and water, salt and pepper. Bring to boil and simmer for 1½-2 hours or until the soup is thick. If desired, halve the soup and liquidize to thicken, then add it to remaining half.

Serve with freshly grated Parmesan cheese and crusty French bread.

CHEF'S TIP: Can be made a few days ahead and refrigerated. Freezes very well.

Serves 10

Basic Chicken Soup and Country Minestrone Soup

BUTTERNUT SOUP

There are hundreds of butternut soup recipes around but I guarantee this is the only one you'll ever turn to as it is both simple to prepare and delicious. PS THIS IS MY BEST SOUP RECIPE EVER!!!!

2	leeks (white only), sliced thinly
30ml (2 T)	butter or margarine
1	large butternut
2	large carrots
2	potatoes
2.5ℓ (10 cups)	water
80ml (⅓ cup)	vegetable or chicken stock powder
250ml (1 cup)	cream – optional

PREPARATION TIME: 15 minutes
COOKING TIME: 1½ hours

Peel and cube butternut, peel and coarsely dice the carrots and potatoes. In a large pot sauté the sliced leeks in butter until soft.

Add the butternut, carrots, potatoes, water and stock cubes to the leeks in the pot. Bring to the boil then simmer on low heat for about 1½ hours. Liquidize the mixture and add cream.

CHEF'S TIP: Reheat on low heat if necessary. Can be frozen in smaller quantities.

I add cream to smooth the texture of the soup. For a lighter option, I add a little extra stock and only ½ cup of yoghurt or cream to the soup.

Serves 8

SPLIT PEA SOUP

A beautiful thick pea soup, this one simply needs many hours of cooking but is fabulously thick and hearty when ready.

4ℓ (16 cups)	water
60ml (4 T)	chicken stock powder
500g (1 lb)	yellow split peas or green split peas, if preferred
2	celery sticks with leaves
2	medium carrots
1	large onion
1	large turnip
	coarse salt
	black pepper

PREPARATION TIME: 20 minutes
COOKING TIME: 2 hours

Place water in a large pot, add the stock powder and the split peas and bring to a boil. Turn the heat to medium low and simmer for 45 minutes.

Cut the celery sticks in half, cut the carrots into chunks, dice the onion and peel and quarter the turnip. Add all the vegetables to the pot and boil gently until all they are tender.

Purée the soup in a liquidizer or with a hand blender. Add additional stock powder if necessary for flavour.

CHEF'S TIP: Soup can be made ahead of time and refrigerated or frozen.

Serves 8-10

Butternut Soup and Split Pea Soup

Chunky Greek Salad

SALADS

The secret to a great salad is the platter on which you serve it. My advice is to buy the freshest, most wonderful-looking vegetables, cut them in different shapes and arrange them on a platter. Dress them with a simple basic salad dressing and you'll be amazed at how it is devoured.

Try to grow your own herbs, either in your garden or in pots on your windowsill – it's rewarding and you'll always have them on hand (plus there's no wastage from store-bought packets).

If you do buy packets of herbs and you want them to last longer, wash then dry them well in a salad spinner, roll in paper towel to remove excess water and store in a sealed plastic bag. This method works well for lettuce too.

LETTUCES

Butter Lettuce

An attractive light green lettuce with soft round leaves and a mild buttery flavour.

Iceberg Lettuce

A popular variety with large crisp leaves and a sweet and slightly watery flavour. Many of us grew up on this salad leaf.

Remember that lettuce should never be cut but rather broken gently.

Cos Lettuce

A Caesar salad staple, this variety has crisp long leaves that are tightly wrapped to form an elongated head and a succulent sweet flavour.

Oak Leaf Lettuce

These leaves have a pretty oak-leaf shape and have a full flavour.

FRENCH SALAD

A simple French salad can be made ahead of time without the dressing as long as the ingredients are not coated with any water as the salad turns brown quickly. Use as few or as many ingredients as you like and only add dressing just before serving. Some suggestions are tomato or cherry tomatoes, cucumber, red onion, celery, peppers, carrots, feta or mozzarella cubes, mushrooms, spring onion, sprouts, avocados and sunflower seeds.

BASIC SALAD DRESSING
The secret to the balance of a dressing is to use 3 parts oil to 1 part vinegar or lemon juice. To this base one can add any extras for flavour. A golden yellow olive oil makes the perfect smooth taste for a dressing.

175ml (¾ cup)	olive oil
60ml (¼ cup)	white spirit vinegar
7.5ml (1½ t)	coarse salt
	black pepper

PREPARATION TIME: 10 minutes

Whisk all the ingredients together and set aside until ready to use.

FANCY SALAD DRESSING

175ml (¾ cup)	olive oil
60ml (¼ cup)	white, red wine or balsamic vinegar
2.5ml (½ t)	dry mustard powder
pinch	sugar
	coarse salt
	black pepper

PREPARATION TIME: 10 minutes

Whisk all ingredients together. Store until ready to use.

CHEF'S TIP: A good quality salad spinner is an essential part of the kitchen to ensure really dry lettuce. A good trick is to put the dressing in the serving bowl, then place the salad ingredients on the top and toss from the bottom.

CABBAGE SALAD

This basic cabbage salad with its creamy dressing is always a winner.

1	whole green cabbage
1	pineapple
2-3	large carrots
250ml (1 cup)	mayonnaise
60ml (¼ cup)	fresh orange juice
10ml (2 t)	sugar
	coarse salt
	black pepper

PREPARATION TIME: 10 minutes

Shred the cabbage very finely. Then grate the pineapple and carrots coarsely and add to the cabbage. Mix all the dressing ingredients together and toss with salad.

Season with salt and pepper to taste.

CHEF'S TIP: Make the salad at least ½ an hour before serving for the cabbage to absorb the dressing and become a little juicy.

Serves 4

CAESAR SALAD

I make a Caesar salad at least once a week in our house as it's top of the list of favourites.

	croutons
3	cos lettuces, broken
	Parmesan, freshly grated

DRESSING

2	egg yolks
4	anchovies (optional)
2.5ml (½ t)	minced garlic
30ml (2 T)	fresh lemon juice
10ml (2 t)	Dijon mustard
160ml (⅔ cup)	light olive oil
2.5ml (½ t)	salt
	black pepper

PREPARATION TIME: 20 minutes

To make the croutons, cut 3 slices of bread into small cubes and either fry or toast them. Set aside.

Place the yolks, anchovies, garlic, lemon juice and mustard in a food processor and process until mixed.

With motor running, drizzle oil through feed tube until dressing is thick and creamy. Season to taste.

Just before serving, pour dressing over lettuce and toss with the croutons and Parmesan.

CHEF'S TIP: I use a light olive oil because I find an extra virgin one too strong for this dressing. Otherwise combine a dark olive oil with sunflower or canola oil. This easy dressing can be made earlier in the day and refrigerated.

Serves 4-6

CHUNKY GREEK SALAD

There's nothing nicer than a chunky salad filled with vegetables and feta. A sprinkle of dry Greek oregano and some dressing completes the picture.

3-4	vine-ripened red tomatoes
1	large English cucumber, deseeded
250g (8 oz)	Greek feta
	Greek Calamata olives
	red onion
	dried oregano
60ml (¼ cup)	olive oil
30ml (2 T)	white wine vinegar
	coarse salt
	black pepper

PREPARATION TIME: 10 minutes

Cut tomatoes, cucumber, feta and red onion into large chunks, place in a bowl and add the remaining ingredients.

Sprinkle with oregano and drizzle with the olive oil and vinegar. A generous teaspoon of coarse salt and some black pepper complete the dish. Toss well just before serving.

CHEF'S TIP: I love adding some chunks of avocado to this salad. Pick the reddest tomatoes available for their sweetness.

Serves 4

Caesar Salad

BASIC POTATO SALAD

This potato salad is a delicious old-fashioned one with chunky potatoes and a tangy creamy dressing.

6	medium potatoes
2	whole spring onions, green and white
3	hard boiled eggs
250ml (1 cup)	mayonnaise
5ml (1 t)	dry mustard powder
5ml (1 t)	white spirit vinegar
	coarse salt
	black pepper

PREPARATION TIME: 35 minutes

Boil the potatoes with their skins. When tender, drain the water, cool and peel. Cut them into cubes and add the spring onions and eggs.

Mix the mayonnaise, mustard, white vinegar, salt and black pepper together. Pour over the potato mixture and toss all ingredients to combine.

CHEF'S TIP: The potatoes absorb the flavour of the dressing the longer it stands.

Serves 6

NIÇOISE SALAD

This makes a wonderful light meal and looks best when arranged simply on a platter.

10	baby potatoes
2	heads butter lettuce
2 x small tins	tuna, drained
3	small ripe tomatoes
1	small red onion
200g (7 oz)	fine French green beans, blanched
6	eggs, hard boiled
	few Calamata olives
	coarse salt
	black pepper
30ml (2 T)	capers, rinsed

DRESSING

175ml (¾ cup)	olive oil
125ml (½ cup)	lemon juice
5ml (1 t)	Dijon mustard
	coarse salt
	black pepper

PREPARATION TIME: 20 minutes

Boil potatoes in salted water until tender, then halve them. Toss with a little dressing while warm and then set aside.

Tear lettuce into pieces and arrange on a serving platter. Mound the tuna in centre of lettuce.

Cut the tomatoes into eighths. Slice the red onion very thinly, quarter the eggs. Arrange them with the green beans, olives and capers in mounds on top of the lettuce. Place the potatoes around the edge. Drizzle entire salad with remaining dressing.

DRESSING
Whisk lemon juice, oil and mustard in a medium bowl. Season with salt and pepper and set aside.

CHEF'S TIP: Most of the ingredients can be prepared ahead and kept refrigerated.

Serves 4

Niçoise Salad

Cannelloni

Buckwheat Noodles

Egg Fettuccine

Fusilli

Penne Tricolore

Farfalle

Extra Fine Noodles

Gnocchetti Sardi

Lasagne

Pasta is not only the most affordable meal option, it's also the easiest to master and tasty in all its forms. You can whip it up when you're craving a homemade meal and even host a pasta dinner for a few friends. If I could eat pasta every day, I would. So how come the Italians eat so much of it and never gain weight? It's just not fair. The secret to great pasta is to use a good quality one and to never overcook it. Otherwise it just becomes stodgy.

Different noodles suit certain sauces better than others, so a heavy-based meat sauce complements spaghetti or rigatoni, whilst fresh pasta is particularly suited to a light sauce or simply tossed with some olive oil, chopped fresh herbs, salt and pepper. Stuffed pastas, such as ravioli and panzerotti are filled with either meat or vegetable fillings and are sold either refrigerated or frozen. If cooking these from the freezer they do not need to be defrosted and can be boiled in the same way as the unfilled variety but should float on the top of the water for at least 5 minutes to cook all the way through. Whichever noodle you use, ensure that it is well coated with the sauce and that the sauce complements rather than overpowers it.

Pasta is a great pantry essential because it can be taken out and cooked in just a few minutes with a simple sauce.

TYPES OF PASTA

Rice Vermicelli

Rosmarino

Pappardelle

Here are some varieties of pasta:

LINGUINE	*thin flat pasta*
FETTUCCINE	*wide flat pasta*
SPAGHETTI	*thin round long pasta*
SPAGHETTINI	*thinner round long pasta*
FUSILLI	*corkscrew pasta*
FARFALLE	*bow-shaped pasta*
PENNE	*tubes cut at an angle*
RIGATONI	*bigger tubes*
CANNELLONI	*large tubes*
LASAGNE	*flat sheets*
MACARONI	*slightly hooked pasta*
CAPELLINI	*very thin angel hair pasta*
ROSMARINO	*rice-shaped pasta*
PAPPARDELLE	*wide flat pasta*
RICE VERMICELLI	*thin rice noodles*

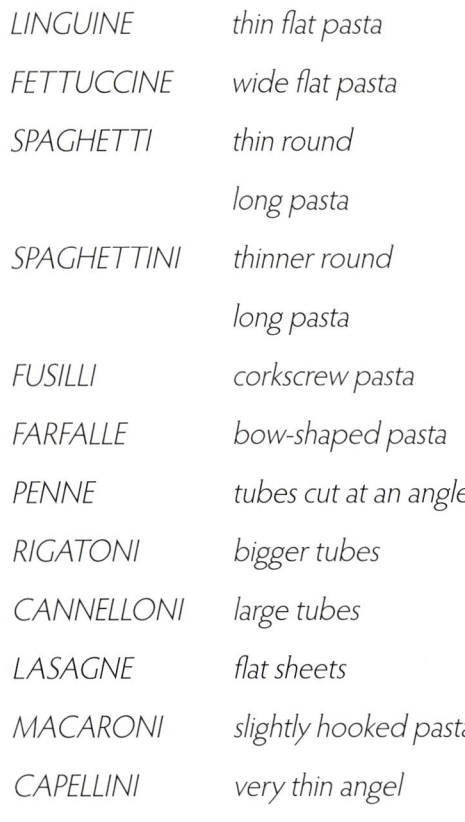

Water plays a vital part in cooking pasta. Cook it in a large pot filled with lots of salted boiling water. As it cooks, it absorbs the water and will stick together if too crowded. Bring the water to a full boil before adding the oil and plenty of salt to taste. Once you have added the pasta to the water, stir it a few times to avoid it sticking but keep the heat on high and cook the pasta "al dente": there should be no white spot left in the centre but it should still have a firm bite. Drain immediately, toss with a drop of olive oil and then add the sauce.

Unless you are using the pasta for a salad or a baked pasta dish where it will continue cooking in the oven, never rinse the pasta with cold water.

I always like to reserve a small amount of the salted cooking water in case it is needed to thin out sauces that are too thick, as it has lots of flavour.

MEAT LASAGNE

Whenever I ask my son what he would like to eat, he always answers meat lasagne. A rich meat sauce is the secret to the special taste.

¾ box	lasagne sheets
	Parmesan, freshly grated

BÉCHAMEL SAUCE

60g (4 T)	butter
60ml (4 T)	flour
625ml (2 ½ cups)	warm milk
	coarse salt
	black pepper
	nutmeg to taste

MEAT SAUCE

250ml (1 cup)	onion
125ml (½ cup)	carrots
125ml (½ cup)	celery
60ml (¼ cup)	olive oil
500g (1 lb)	lean ground beef
2 x 410g (14 oz)	tins Italian chopped tomatoes
250ml (1 cup)	beef stock
30ml (2 T)	tomato paste
1	bay leaf
5ml (1 tsp)	dried oregano
	coarse salt
	black pepper
10ml (2 t)	sugar

PREPARATION TIME: 30 minutes
COOKING TIME: 50-60 minutes

BÉCHAMEL SAUCE

Melt the butter in a medium pot. Add flour and cook for 3 minutes. Pour in the warmed milk and whisk occasionally for 3-5 minutes until thickened and lightly coating the back of a spoon. Season to taste with salt, pepper and nutmeg. Set aside.

MEAT SAUCE

Chop the onions, carrots and celery in a food processor. Sauté in large pan with olive oil, stirring occasionally for 5 minutes until softened. Then add the ground beef in batches, cooking a little at a time for the water to evaporate. Add the tomatoes, beef stock, tomato paste, bay leaf, oregano, salt and pepper to taste. Cover and simmer 1 hour. Adjust seasoning and add sugar.

Preheat oven to 180° C.

Spray an ovenproof dish with non-stick cooking spray. Spread a layer of the meat sauce evenly over the bottom of the dish. Top with a layer of lasagne sheets. Then add 1 cup of the béchamel sauce, smoothing it over the lasagne. Continue layering with meat sauce, lasagne and béchamel sauce, ending with béchamel sauce. Sprinkle top with Parmesan cheese. Cover with foil. Place in oven and bake covered for 30 minutes. Remove foil and continue baking for another 20 minutes or until lasagne feels soft when pricked with a fork.

CHEF'S TIP: I like to make it and keep it refrigerated until I am ready to bake it which also softens the lasagne sheets.

Precooked lasagne sheets are quite thick and hard and require a lot of liquid when cooking in order to soften them. Resting the lasagne for a few hours before baking will soften the sheets but always ensure that they are well covered with liquid.

Serves 6

FETTUCCINE WITH MUSHROOM CREAM SAUCE

A classic pasta well worth the kilojoules.

350g (9½ oz)	fettuccine
250g (8 oz)	mushrooms, sliced

BÉCHAMEL SAUCE

45ml (3 T)	butter
15ml (1 T)	flour
625ml (2½ cups)	low fat milk
250ml (1 cup)	cream
15ml (1 T)	Herbamare
	coarse salt
	black pepper
	Parmesan, freshly grated

PREPARATION TIME: 10 minutes
COOKING TIME: 20 minutes

Sauté the sliced mushrooms in a medium pot without any butter or oil until softened and browned but not dry. Set aside.

In the same pot make a béchamel sauce.

Melt the butter, then stir in the flour and cook for 1 minute. Slowly whisk in the milk, removing any lumps. Add the cream, Herbamare, salt and pepper to taste. Lastly add the cooked mushrooms.

Toss the sauce with the fettuccine. Sprinkle with lots of black pepper and top with the Parmesan.

CHEF'S TIP: This sauce is not made with cream but a thin béchamel which only has some cream added (so the fat content is lower). If necessary add a little extra milk to thin it out so as not to make the pasta stodgy. The sauce can be refrigerated or frozen and reheated.

Serves 4

LINGUINE WITH TOMATO BASIL SAUCE

Fresh basil is a must in this classic sauce, while a drop of cream will do wonders in smoothing out the tomato.

400g (9 oz)	linguine or penne
1	onion
5ml (1 t)	fresh minced garlic
80ml (⅓ cup)	olive oil
2 x 410g (14 oz)	tins whole peeled tomatoes
30ml (2 T)	sugar
30ml (2 T)	fresh basil
	coarse salt
	black pepper
60ml (¼ cup)	cream (optional)

PREPARATION TIME: 10 minutes
COOKING TIME: 20 minutes

Finely chop the onion. Heat the olive oil in a medium pot and fry the onion and garlic on medium heat until soft and golden. Process the tomatoes with the liquid in a processor, then add them to the pot and simmer uncovered on medium-low heat for 20 minutes or until thickened. Stir in the sugar, salt and pepper. Add cream if desired. Sprinkle with freshly ground black pepper.

Cook pasta "al dente". Drain and toss with the sauce. Cut the basil into small pieces. Add to the pasta. Sprinkle with a little more freshly ground black pepper and serve immediately.

CHEF'S TIP: This sauce freezes well without the basil – only add the basil after reheating.

Serves 4

Tomato Basil Sauce and Mushroom Cream Sauce

PENNE WITH CREAMY TOMATO SAUCE

A tasty and easy dish that goes well with salad and some crusty bread.

500g (1 lb)	penne or rigatoni
60ml (¼ cup)	olive oil
10ml (2 t)	fresh minced garlic
2.5ml (½ t)	fresh minced chilli
2 x 410g (14 oz)	tins Italian chopped tomatoes
60ml (¼ cup)	vodka (optional)
125ml (½ cup)	thick cream
	coarse salt
	black pepper
10ml (2 t)	sugar

PREPARATION TIME: 20 minutes
COOKING TIME: 20 minutes

Heat the garlic in olive oil in a medium pot. Add the chilli, simmer for a few minutes and then add the chopped tomatoes. Simmer for about 15 minutes uncovered.

Then pour in the vodka and cream and simmer for a little longer or until thickened. Add salt, pepper and sugar to taste.

Cook the pasta "al dente".

Toss with the sauce and serve immediately.

CHEF'S TIP: Add a little Parmesan and some chopped parsley for a little more flavour. The sauce freezes well, so make an extra batch if desired and freeze.

Serves 4-6

MACARONI CHEESE

A very simple pasta dish with lots of flavour and a tangy sauce.

500g (1 lb)	elbow macaroni

CHEESE SAUCE

90g (6 T)	butter or margarine
60ml (¼ cup)	flour
1ℓ (4 cups)	warm milk
625ml (2 ½ cups)	cheddar cheese
5ml (1 t)	nutmeg
	coarse salt
	black pepper

PREPARATION TIME: 15 minutes
COOKING TIME: 30 minutes

Boil the macaroni until slightly undercooked Set aside. Preheat oven to 180° C.

CHEESE SAUCE
Melt the butter in a large pot. Stir in the flour and cook for 1 minute. Pour the warmed milk in slowly and whisk until thickened. Season with salt and pepper and sprinkle with nutmeg. Remove from stove and stir in ¾ of the cheese until melted. Toss together with the cooked macaroni.

Place the mixture in a large sprayed ovenproof dish. Sprinkle with remaining cheddar and bake on the middle rack of the oven for about 30 minutes or until bubbling and golden.

CHEF'S TIP: This dish can be prepared ahead and refrigerated until ready to bake. Bake just before serving for best results. The sauce can be used over cauliflower to make cauliflower au gratin.

Serves 6

Penne With Creamy Tomato Sauce

SPAGHETTI BOLOGNESE

I don't know anyone who doesn't love a good spaghetti Bolognese. This recipe calls for carrots for added sweetness and colour. If there are any leftovers, why not make a sloppy Joe on soft white rolls – my kids love it.

200g (7.5 oz)	spaghetti
2	large carrots
1	onion
30ml (2 T)	olive oil
500g (1 lb)	extra lean beef mince
2 x 410g (14 oz)	tins Italian chopped tomatoes
10ml (2 t)	sugar
5ml (1 t)	dry oregano
5ml (1 t)	dry sweet basil
60ml (¼ cup)	tomato sauce
	coarse salt
	black pepper

PREPARATION TIME: 15-20 minutes
COOKING TIME: 1 hour

Finely chop carrots and onion in a food processor. Heat olive oil and then sauté carrots and onion in the olive oil in a medium pot until softened. Cook the meat in small batches, mashing gently to remove lumps. Once all the mince has been added, stir in the tomatoes, sugar, oregano and basil.

Reduce heat to medium-low, cover and simmer gently covered for about 1 hour. Add the tomato sauce and season with salt and pepper.

Cook spaghetti "al dente", drain off water and then toss with a drop of olive oil before tossing with the meat sauce so that the sauce coats the pasta.

CHEF'S TIP: I like adding tomato sauce for a little bit of extra sweetness and to thicken the sauce. The sauce freezes very well.

Serves 4-6

Spaghetti Bolognese

Quick Oven Fish Dish

Fish is very healthy, especially fatty fish such as salmon and tuna which are full of heart-healthy Omega 3.

When buying fish, it's important that it's very fresh. Look for fish with beautifully coloured flesh, a shiny and wet skin and black, not grey eyes. Always buy fish that's in season and that you can afford.

For the sake of the environment, we need to be aware of what fish species are endangered and commit to not buying or consuming them (check the Internet for more info on what fish are sustainable).

Ask your fishmonger to do the required cutting, scaling and filleting – it's much easier than doing it yourself.

A good guide to learning the cooking time of fish is:

Cook fish 10 minutes for every 1 cm of thickness example, a fish that is 2 cm thick will take 20 minutes exactly. This works for any piece of fish and for whichever method you choose to prepare it. Another great tip is to pierce the fish with a fork and when there is no resistance and the fork pierces easily, the fish is cooked.

Mock Crayfish

Grilled Linefish

Quick Oven Fish Dish

Salmon Fish Cakes

Fried Fish

MOCK CRAYFISH

Unfortunately when making mock crayfish what looks like a lot of raw fish doesn't look like that much when it has been cooked as it seems to shrink quite a bit. For this recipe I prefer to use kingklip which is a much firmer fish.

1kg (2.2 lbs)	hake or kingklip fillets

SAUCE

175ml (¾ cup)	mayonnaise
125ml (½ cup)	tomato sauce
5ml (1 t)	Worcestershire sauce
15ml (1 T)	lemon juice
	few drops of Tabasco
	coarse salt
	black pepper

PREPARATION TIME: 10 minutes
COOKING TIME: 35 minutes

Place fish in a medium pot filled with cold water. Season the water with a little salt and a squeeze of lemon juice. Bring the water to a boil, lower heat to medium and simmer fish with lid on for about 15-20 minutes or until fish is firm and cooked. Pour off water and drain in a strainer.

Set aside to cool and then break into pieces.

SAUCE

Mix all ingredients together then toss over the fish. To serve, place a few spoonfuls in avocado halves on a bed of lettuce. Place on a small platter and decorate with parsley, lemon and sliced egg.

Serves 4

GRILLED LINEFISH

There are two ways to grill fish – either under the grill in the oven or in a pan on the stove. Grilling produces a more succulent fish but when cooking a large piece of fish, grilling in the oven is preferable as it's easier to handle. A little bit of olive oil is the only fat you need for cooking, while keeping the skin on keeps the flesh intact.

1kg (2.2 lb)	linefish – kabeljou, Cape salmon – filleted with skin
	olive oil
	Herbamare
	coarse salt
	black pepper
	Italian parsley, freshly chopped

OVEN GRILLING

Preheat the grill. Line a baking tray with foil or a non-stick liner.

Rub the skin with a little olive oil, season with Herbamare, coarse salt and black pepper. Place fish skin-side down and repeat procedure, seasoning well.

Place fish on middle rack directly under the grill with door slightly ajar (this keeps the top element red, which is essential for grilling).
Grill for 15-20 minutes or until quite dark brown, without turning. Pierce with a fork to test if cooked.

PAN GRILLING

Preheat a ridged grilling pan until quite hot. Spray pan with olive oil spray. Then place fish, flesh side down in the pan and grill for about 5 minutes without turning. Turn over and cook for another 5 minutes. Turn again, lower heat. and then grill for a further 8-10 minutes or until cooked through.

CHEF'S TIP: Allow 250g linefish portion per person.

Serves 4

Grilled Linefish

QUICK OVEN FISH DISH

This is a simple dish but an all-time favourite

1kg (2.2 lb)	hake, kingklip or any linefish
500ml (2 cups)	any light Italian Salad dressing
125g (4 oz)	packet salt and vinegar chips

PREPARATION TIME: 8 minutes
COOKING TIME: 25 minutes

Preheat oven to 180° C.

Spray an ovenproof dish with non-stick spray. Place fish in the dish, tucking the thin narrow end underneath to ensure even cooking. Pour over the salad dressing.

Crush the chips inside the packet and sprinkle over the fish. Bake on middle rack of oven uncovered for about 25 minutes or until golden.

CHEF'S TIP: Stock fish is perfect for this dish, as it can be baked longer if necessary for colour.

Serves 4

SALMON FISH CAKES

Delicious for dinner or a light lunch with a side salad.

415g (14½ oz)	tin pink salmon
15ml (1 T)	wholegrain mustard
15ml (1 T)	mayonnaise
15ml (1 T)	pickled cucumber
15ml (1 T)	Italian parsley
15ml (1 T)	baby salad onions
1	whole egg
30ml (2 T)	matzo meal or breadcrumbs (+ extra for coating fish cakes)
	coarse salt
	black pepper

LEMON MAYONNAISE SAUCE

30ml (1 T)	fresh lemon juice
30ml (2 T)	mayonnaise
30ml (2 T)	water
	coarse salt
	black pepper

PREPARATION TIME: 15 minutes
COOKING TIME: 10 minutes

Drain, clean and flake the pink salmon. Chop the pickled cucumber, Italian parsley and salad onions and then mix all the ingredients together in a large bowl.

Heat a little sunflower oil in a shallow frying pan. Shape fish into medium rounds and then dip into either matzo meal or breadcrumbs. Fry on medium heat on both sides until golden brown.

Drain on paper towel. Serve slightly warmed with Lemon Mayonnaise Sauce.

LEMON MAYONNAISE SAUCE
Whisk all above ingredients together and drizzle over the fish cakes just before serving.

CHEF'S TIP: Place the fried fish cakes on a baking rack to cool and use the same rack to reheat them in a low 140° C oven for about 5-8 minutes to warm them through.

Make 8-10 fish cakes

Salmon Fish Cakes

FRIED FISH

I use two methods for frying fish, the first of which produces a much crisper result. The ideal fish for frying are hake, kingklip and sole.

METHOD 1 – CRUMBS

Flour, seasoned generously with coarse salt
    and pepper
1 egg, lightly beaten with some water
1 cup breadcrumbs or medium matzo meal

Dip fish first into flour, then egg and then breadcrumbs. Leave to rest for a few minutes uncovered on a board before frying.

METHOD 2 – FLOUR

1 egg, lightly beaten with some water
Flour, seasoned generously with coarse salt
    and pepper

Dip fish first into egg, then into the flour. Fry immediately, no resting required

When frying, always fry in sunflower or canola oil that is at least 2-cm deep. There's no need for deep-frying. Heat the oil first until quite hot, as fish will brown quickly and will not absorb all the oil. Lower the heat if necessary depending on the type and thickness of the fish, so as not to burn the crumbs. Fish should not be fried for longer than 20 minutes in total. However, stock fish, such as hake, can fry for any amount of time as it will never become hard.

To check readiness of fish, prick with a fork, which should pierce through easily. Drain the fish on paper towel and/or brown paper to remove the excess oil. Once cool, leave fish uncovered on a rack to prevent it becoming soggy. Reheat in a very low oven for a few minutes if you prefer to serve it warm.

A wedge of lemon and a little mayonnaise make a great accompaniment.

Fried Fish

Spatchcock Grilled Baby Chickens

POULTRY

Before you start cooking a chicken, buying one is important – if organic, free-range chickens are available, then it would be wise to start there. They are tastier and healthier and are reared on open farms free from antibiotics and hormones.

A few years ago, I invested in a good quality grilling pan This very sturdy pan only requires a little olive oil cooking spray and high heat. So when I grill chicken breasts, they are seared on the outside and juicy inside. Lean chicken breasts tend to dry out quickly, so they should be cooked and eaten immediately. It's the same with a roast chicken. It takes exactly 90 minutes from start to finish for a perfectly gorgeous, well-basted chicken. You can then be assured of a succulent bird.

I like roasting on a high temperature of at least 180° C or even 200° C on the bottom rack of the oven. Shake the pan periodically to prevent the skin sticking to the roasting pan. Add a little water to the roasting pan to turn the natural juices into a perfect gravy.

Guide for poultry cooking times to achieve the perfect result:

1 Whole chicken: 90 minutes

Chicken pieces: 45 minutes

Chicken breasts with skin and bone: 30 minutes

Chicken breast fillets: 20 minutes

1 Whole turkey: approximately 3-3 ½ hours

CHICKEN CURRY

A delicate blend of spicy and sweet make this curry a firm favourite. It can just as easily be made with lamb or beef knuckles. Adding vegetables will give a lovely colour to the dish while an assortment of sambals such as coconut, banana, pineapple, tomato and onion make it the perfect meal.

4	onions, sliced
60ml (¼ cup)	olive oil
2	chickens
175ml (¾ cup)	smooth apricot jam
45ml (3 T)	medium curry powder
4	bay leaves
125ml (½ cup)	white vinegar
375ml (1½ cups)	water
30ml (2 T)	chicken stock powder
	coarse salt
	black pepper
3	carrots, cut into thick slices
2	potatoes, peeled and quartered

PREPARATION TIME: 25 minutes
COOKING TIME: 1 hour

Heat olive oil and then fry onions in a large pot until browned. Set aside.

Cut the chickens into large pieces and season them with salt and pepper. Brown the chicken in batches in the same pot until nicely golden – you won't need to add more oil as the chicken skin will provide ample fat. Pour off any excess oil during the browning process.

Return onions to pot, adding all remaining ingredients and simmer on medium heat without the lid on for at least 1 hour.

Remove chicken pieces, continue to boil sauce until it thickens nicely and then pour over chicken to coat. Before serving, boil some carrot pieces and quartered potatoes and add to curry.

*I like using store brands of curry powder, there are so many on the market. Your local Indian market can mix the spices for you.

CHEF'S TIP: The chickens need a maximum of 1 hour's cooking or they will be overcooked. If you would like to freeze, do not cook the vegetables with the chicken but rather before serving.

Serves 8

ROAST WHOLE CHICKEN

This fabulous roast chicken recipe will become a favourite. It should be roasted on the bottom rack for maximum colour and crispiness. I just love the skin – it's the best part.

1	whole chicken
	juice of 1 lemon
	seasoning salt (see below)
	black pepper
125ml (½ cup)	boiling water

SEASONING SALT

10ml (2 t)	dry herbs for chicken
5ml (1 t)	coarse salt
15ml (1 T)	chicken seasoning
15ml (1 T)	fresh rosemary
5ml (1 t)	Herbamare

PREPARATION TIME: 10 minutes
COOKING TIME: 90 minutes

Preheat oven to 180° C.

Mix all seasonings together and set aside.

Spray a roasting pan with non-stick spray. Wash chicken inside and out. Pat dry. Squeeze juice of lemon all over the chicken.

Sprinkle with seasoning salt and black pepper. Roast on bottom rack for 45 minutes. Turn chicken over, season other side and roast for a further 45 minutes breast side up.

CHEF'S TIP: Keep shaking the pan all the time to prevent the skin from sticking to the roasting pan.

Serves 4-6

Chicken Curry

SPATCHCOCK GRILLED BABY CHICKENS

This is one of those dishes that is so delicious you'll want to eat it straight from the oven! It's such a hit with my family that I always make extra!

4	potatoes, quartered and boiled
30ml (2 T)	olive oil
15ml (1 T)	sweet paprika
15ml (1 T)	seasoning salt
10ml (2 t)	coarse salt
	black pepper
4	baby chickens, spatch-cocked and flattened *
60ml (¼ cup)	Italian parsley , freshly chopped

*A spatchcock chicken is one that has been cut down the backbone and flattened. This allows the flavour to coat all sides of the chicken. If you would like to use 2 whole regular size chickens instead of 4 baby chickens, cooking time will be 90 minutes in total.

PREPARATION TIME: 10 minutes
COOKING TIME: 70 minutes

Preheat oven to 200° C. Place quartered potatoes around the sides of a large roasting pan. Mix all the seasonings together. Drizzle the potatoes with olive oil and sprinkle with some seasoning.

Cut the chickens down the centre of the backbone to spatchcock them and rub seasoning all over. Place them in the centre of the roasting pan skin side down and roast on the middle rack of the oven for about 40 minutes. Turn the potatoes over halfway during the cooking.

Preheat the grill. Place the roasting pan on the lowest rack of the oven and grill for about 15 minutes. Check the potatoes and when done, remove them from the oven so that they don't burn. Turn the chickens over to face skin side up and grill for another 15 minutes, watching carefully that they don't burn. Sprinkle with Italian parsley just before serving, and surround with the potatoes.

CHEF'S TIP: I like to roast the chickens first for 40 minutes and then grill them for the remainder of the time but they will burn if too close to the grill, which is why you need to move them to the bottom of the oven. The potatoes should be almost cooked after the first 40 minutes. As soon as they are ready, remove them from the roasting pan and keep them warm. Sweet paprika is available at speciality shops.

Serves 4

CHICKEN SCHNITZELS

These bring back so many memories of my trips to Europe, where schnitzels are a very popular Swiss dish. These are quick to prepare and even quicker to cook.

6	chicken fillets
125ml (½ cup)	flour
	coarse salt
	black pepper
1	egg, lightly beaten with some water
375ml (1½ cups)	cornflake crumbs
	Sunflower oil and grape seed oil for frying

PREPARATION TIME: 25 minutes
COOKING TIME: 10 minutes

Pound the chicken fillets with a mallet* to break the sinew and flatten them. Dip each one into the seasoned flour, then the beaten egg and then the cornflake crumbs. Place on an open board in the fridge for about 15 minutes to set the crumbs.

Meanwhile, heat a little oil in a medium frying pan (I mix sunflower and grape seed). The oil should be quite shallow. Deep-frying is not necessary. Brown on medium high heat on each side for about 5-6 minutes.

Drain on paper towel and then keep uncovered on a flat platter. Warm for a few minutes just before serving with some lemon wedges

*A kitchen tool like a hammer

CHEF'S TIP: Chicken schnitzels can be replaced with veal schnitzels. When they are very thin, they will only require about 8 minutes of cooking in total.

Serves 4

Chicken Schnitzels

GRILLED BALSAMIC CHICKEN BREASTS

This dish is easy to prepare and very handy when short of time and the family is big on appetite! The higher the heat, the quicker the chicken will grill and the more coloured they'll be. Great for everyday!

8	chicken fillets
80ml (⅓ cup)	olive oil
80ml (⅓ cup)	balsamic vinegar
	juice of 1 orange
15ml (1 T)	syrup or honey
	coarse salt
	black pepper

PREPARATION TIME: 10 minutes
COOKING TIME: 15 minutes

Pound each chicken fillet with a mallet*. Place them in a Ziploc bag and marinate in the olive oil, balsamic vinegar and black pepper for ½ an hour before grilling. Only season with the salt just before grilling.

Remove fillets from the bag and pour the marinade into a small pot. Add the orange juice and syrup and boil on high heat, reducing slightly.

Heat a grilling pan on high. Grill fillets on each side for about 5 minutes or until just cooked through, brushing them with the marinade during cooking. Remove from the grill when ready.

*Kitchen tool like a hammer

CHEF'S TIP: Because the grilling pan is direct heat, the chicken fillets cook very quickly.

Serves 6

ROAST TURKEY

Roasting a turkey is not as daunting a task as it seems. I first like to get the turkey golden brown and then add sauces and flavours for the last hour to ensure a succulent, juicy bird.

4-5kg (10 lb)	turkey
30ml (2 T)	seasoning salt
	coarse salt
	black pepper
1	onion, cut into 4
2	carrots, into large pieces
few	sprigs of rosemary
few	sprigs of sage
handful	Italian parsley
30ml (2 T)	olive oil
375ml (1½ cups)	water

PREPARATION TIME: 20 minutes
COOKING TIME: 3-3 ½ hours

Preheat oven to 200° C.

Rub inside of turkey with lots of salt and pepper and some seasoning salt. Place the onion, carrots, rosemary, sage and parsley in cavity. Tie legs together with some string. Drizzle a drop of olive oil over the outside of the turkey and season well with more salt, pepper and seasoning salt.

Place the turkey breast-side down on a rack in a roasting pan so that the juices drip into the pan. Place on the bottom rack and roast uncovered until crisp and golden, turning after the first hour.

After 2 hours add 375ml (1½ cups) water to the roasting pan. Place the turkey in the roasting pan

and baste with the juices that have collected at the bottom. Roast for another hour or until golden and glazed, turning to colour both sides. Rest for 15 minutes before carving.

CHEF'S TIP: To check if the turkey is cooked, pierce the leg/thigh with the fork. If the juices run clear, it's cooked.

Serves 10-12

Turkey sizes:
5.5-7kg (12-15 lb) turkey for 10-12 people
7-8kg (15-18 lb) turkey for 14-16 people
8-10kg (18-22 lb) turkey for 20-22 people

Grilled Balsamic Chicken Breasts

Roast Leg Of Lamb

When buying meat, it's important that your menu is designed around what is available and fresh – develop a good relationship with your butcher who will not only advise you on cuts and cooking times but can do any filleting, cutting and deboning to your liking.

Cooking times:

15-20 minutes per 500g for medium rare

20-25 minutes per 500g for medium

25-30 minutes per 500g for well-done

This applies to most meats, except fillet – because fillet is so thin, it won't ever take longer than 30 minutes, especially for medium-rare in the middle.

Here are a few tips for choosing a good piece of meat:

Meat that is a deeper red is a good indication that the meat is mature and tender. A small piece of fat along the side is ideal for grilling.

Tenderize your meat by rubbing some olive oil on it and leaving it covered in the fridge for a few days as the oil breaks down the sinew in the meat.

Roast Leg Of Lamb

Classic Roast Beef

Old-Fashioned Lamb Stew

Steak and Chops

Beef Casserole

Cottage Pie

Homemade Hamburger Patties

ROAST LEG OF LAMB

There is nothing heartier than a soft, melt-in-the mouth lamb roast where the meat is tender and juicy.

1.5kg (3.3 lb)	leg of lamb
60ml (¼ cup)	olive oil
125ml (½ cup)	fresh lemon juice
30ml (2 T)	fresh rosemary, chopped
60ml (4 T)	fresh oregano, chopped
250ml (1 cup)	water
30ml (2 T)	beef stock powder
	coarse salt
	black pepper

PREPARATION TIME: 15 minutes
COOKING TIME: 2 hours

Preheat oven to 160° C.

Spray a small roasting pan with non-stick cooking spray. Rub roast with olive oil, lemon juice, herbs, salt and pepper. Place in the roasting pan. Cover with foil and place in oven.

Keep roast covered with foil for 2 hours, turning after 1 hour. Then remove the foil, dissolve the beef stock powder in the cup of boiling water, add it to the roasting pan and brown roast for another hour. Season further if necessary. Slice meat and leave in the sauce to keep it juicy.

CHEF'S TIP: This recipe works very well with shoulder of lamb as well, but you might need to buy 2 as there are a lot of bones. I would also increase the lemon juice and stock. When reheating, ensure that the meat is covered with sauce so as not to dry out.

Serves 4-6

CLASSIC ROAST BEEF

I'm amazed that something as simple as salad dressing can penetrate a roast and add so much flavour. A little fat on the meat is important to keep it juicy.

2kg (4.4 lb)	topside roast, sirloin or Scotch fillet
60ml (¼ cup)	mixed freshly chopped herbs - oregano, thyme, basil
1	bottle low fat Italian salad dressing
	coarse salt
	black pepper

PREPARATION TIME: 15 minutes
COOKING TIME: 1 hour 15 minutes

Pour dressing and herbs over the meat and keep in a sealed bag for 24 hours before cooking. Do not season with any salt as this draws the blood out of the meat. Remove the roast from the marinade just before roasting.

Preheat oven to 200° C.

Spray a roasting pan with non-stick spray. Place the roast in the roasting pan, season well with coarse salt and pepper and roast without any marinade for 40 minutes.

Turn meat then pour over half of the marinade and roast for another 15 minutes. Turn and pour over the remaining marinade and roast for another 10 minutes. Remove from oven, cover with foil and rest for 10 minutes then carve.

*The colour of the juice running out of a roast when pricked with a fork, will indicate how much the meat has roasted.

Clear = well done
Light pink = medium
Red = medium rare

CHEF'S TIP: Always allow meat to rest covered for 10 minutes before carving. This allows the juices to settle and makes it easier to carve.

Serves 8-10

Classic Roast Beef

OLD-FASHIONED LAMB STEW

A really hearty lamb stew, this recipe can be cooked for hours until the meat is very soft. It makes a great winter dish.

2	onions, sliced thinly
45ml (3 T)	olive oil
2kg (4.4 lbs)	lamb neck and knuckles
2 x 410g (14 oz)	tins whole peeled tomatoes
375 ml (1½ cups)	water
15ml (1 T)	beef stock powder
10ml (2 t)	oregano
10ml (2 t)	sugar
10ml (2 t)	sweet basil
	coarse salt
	black pepper
	carrots
	potatoes
	peas
	button mushrooms

PREPARATION TIME: 25 minutes
COOKING TIME: 2-3 hours

Fry onions in olive oil until golden and brown. Remove with a slotted spoon and set aside. In the same oil, brown meat which has been seasoned with salt and pepper on both sides until very brown. Do not overcrowd your pot.

Return onions to pot when all the meat has been browned. Liquidize the tomatoes with the juice, dissove the stock powder in the boiling water and add to the pot with the oregano, basil and sugar. Allow to simmer for at least 2-3 hours, covered or until meat is very soft. Only season with salt and pepper at the end of the cooking time.

If the sauce is not thick enough, increase the heat slightly and reduce, uncovered, to thicken. Only add vegetables after 2 hours of cooking or ¾ hr before serving as they collapse.

Vegetables to add: Sliced carrots – boiled until just soft; quartered potatoes – cooked in water for about 15-20 minutes; peas and button mushrooms.

CHEF'S TIP: This freezes very well but exclude the potatoes.

Serves 6

STEAK AND CHOPS

The secret to a juicy steak is to seal it first.

1 kg (2.2 lbs)	rump, porterhouse, fillet, T-bone steak
15ml (1 T)	olive oil
	coarse salt
	black pepper
10ml (2 t)	seasoning salt

PREPARATION TIME: 2 minutes
COOKING TIME: 8-10 minutes

Heat a frying or grilling pan on high until smoky. Rub a drop of olive oil onto the pan. Season meat and then sear on one side for about 5 minutes. Turn over and sear the other side for another 5 minutes, lowering heat to avoid burning.

COOKING TIMES:
Medium rare – 5 minutes each side
Medium – 8-10 minutes each side
Well done – 10-12 minutes each side

LOIN OR RIB CHOPS: These are the tenderest cuts for grilling. Season exactly as for steak, but grill on medium-high heat, turning frequently after searing to cook through. A chop should be cooked medium for serving.

CHEF'S TIP: A small piece of fat along one side of a steak or chops is essential for moisture on the meat when grilling to prevent it from becoming dry. Allow approx. 200-250g per person.

Serves 4-6

Old-Fashioned Lamb Stew

BEEF CASSEROLE

This simple casserole can be made early in the day and reheated very successfully. The longer it cooks the more flavoursome it will be. I prefer cutting the meat into large chunks because they shrink when they cook for a long time.

1.5kg (3.3 lbs)	topside roast or bolo roast
2	onions
2	large carrots,
45ml (3 T)	olive oil
250ml (1 cup)	red wine
500ml (2 cups)	boiling water
45ml (3 T)	beef stock powder
410g (14 oz)	tin Italian chopped tomatoes
15ml (1 T)	sugar
15ml (1 T)	thyme
15ml (1 T)	oregano
2	bay leaves
2	medium potatoes
250g (8 oz)	whole white mushrooms
250ml (1 cup)	fresh or frozen baby carrots
30ml (2 T)	Maizena

PREPARATION TIME: 25 minutes
COOKING TIME: 3 hours

Cut meat into large chunks (approximately 3cm).

Slice the onions thinly. Coarsely chop the carrots. Then fry the carrots and onions in a heavy bottomed pot in olive oil until softened. Set aside. In same pot on high heat, season meat with salt and pepper and fry in small batches until nicely browned, adding more oil if necessary to prevent burning. Set aside once browned.

Add wine to pot and reduce for 1 minute. Dissolve the beef stock powder in the boiling water and add to the pot with the tomatoes, sugar, thyme, oregano and bay leaves. Place meat, onions and carrots back in pot and simmer, covered for at least 3 hours or until meat is very soft.

Dissolve the Maizena in a little cold water and then add to rapidly boiling sauce to thicken it if necessary. Season with salt and pepper to taste.

Peel and cut the potatoes into large cubes. Add them for the last 45 minutes of cooking. Add whole mushrooms and fresh or frozen baby carrots 30 minutes after the potatoes.

CHEF'S TIP: Freezes well without the vegetables.

Serves 4-6

Beef Casserole

COTTAGE PIE

A great alternative to the mashed potato topping is mashed squash which can be prepared in the same way.

1	onion, chopped
60ml (4 T)	olive oil
1kg (2.2 lbs)	beef, veal or chicken mince
250ml (1 cup)	boiling water
30ml (2 T)	beef stock powder
125ml (½ cup)	tomato purée
60ml (4 T)	breadcrumbs
	coarse salt
	black pepper

MASH POTATO

700g (1.5 lb)	baking potatoes, peeled and halved
60ml (4 T)	butter or margarine
60ml (¼ cup)	milk or water
	coarse salt
	black pepper

PREPARATION TIME: 25 minutes
COOKING TIME: 30 minutes

Heat the olive oil then fry onion in a medium pot until golden. Add mince and brown in batches. Add stock and tomato purée to pot and simmer on low heat until slightly thickened but still juicy. Season to taste.

Preheat the oven to 180° C. Spray an ovenproof dish with non-stick spray, place the meat in it and top with mashed potatoes. Sprinkle some breadcrumbs over the mashed potatoes and bake in the oven for about 30 minutes or until golden.

MASH POTATO

Boil potatoes until soft in salted water. When soft, drain the potatoes, reserving about ½ - ¾ cup water. Mash potatoes with a fork or potato masher. Add the milk, butter and seasoning. Continue mixing until fluffy and smooth, adding some of the reserved water if necessary.

CHEF'S TIP: Can be reheated in the microwave.

Serves 4

HOMEMADE HAMBURGER PATTIES

I love a homemade beef hamburger patty because it is plump, juicy and oozing with flavour.

500g (1 lb)	extra lean beef mince
30ml (2 T)	Italian parsley, chopped
15ml (1 T)	Worcestershire sauce
15ml (1 T)	seasoning salt
15ml (1 T)	soya sauce
1	egg, lightly beaten
30ml (2 T)	breadcrumbs
15ml (1 T)	sweet chilli sauce
	coarse salt
	black pepper

PREPARATION TIME: 10 minutes
COOKING TIME: 15 minutes

Mix all ingredients together and shape into large patties. Lightly brush each patty with some olive oil and refrigerate until ready to use. Spray a ridged grilling pan or non-stick frying pan with olive oil spray and heat on medium-high heat. Grill patties on both sides until well-browned and cooked through.

CHEF'S TIP: A great idea for serving these is to spread some crusty rolls with mashed avocado. Then top with the hamburger patty and a tangy onion and tomato sauce in true South African fashion. The patties can be frozen uncooked, defrosted and then grilled.

Makes 4-5 patties

Cottage Pie

Stir-Fry Vegetables

Vegetables are vital ingredients to add to a dish because of their colour, taste, texture and nutritional value. Choose them in season, when they're at their freshest, tastiest and most nutritious. Look for crisp vegetables with brightly coloured leaves, firm skins and unblemished flesh.

WHOLE BUTTERNUT IN THE MICROWAVE

When I was just starting to cook, I learnt this method of cooking butternut in a microwave and it is foolproof. The size of the butternut will determine the length of cooking time, so it's a good idea to undercook rather than overcook it, as it dries out on the ends.

Cut a small cone at the largest point of the butternut.

Fill the hole with 15-30ml (1-2 T) of water. Replace cone loosely. Place the butternut on a plate inside a packet and loosely tie the ends.

Cook on high for 15 minutes. Feel butternut. If a little hard, then continue cooking for another 5 minutes. Remove from packet.

Slice in half and scoop out the pips. Season and fluff the insides.

METHODS OF COOKING VEGETABLES

STEAMING

Steaming is a wonderful way to cook most vegetables because it is so gentle. It allows them to retain more of their shape, colour, texture, flavour and nutrition. Bring the water to a boil before adding the vegetables to the basket and make sure the water in your pan doesn't touch the bottom of the steamer basket. Cover and cook. Ensure the water doesn't boil away, adding more boiling water to the pan as necessary.

BLANCHING

Blanching is an easy technique that is used to keep vegetables crisp and tender. Bring water to a boil in pot over high heat. Add some salt which brings out the flavour, then add the vegetable. Cover with a lid, bring the water to a boil again and time it from when it has reboiled. When the vegetable is firm yet tender, remove from the pot and place immediately into ice water. This preserves the colour, texture and flavour. When cold, remove them from the water, dry thoroughly on a towel.

ROASTING

Roasting vegetables is an excellent low fat cooking method. They should be cut evenly and spread in a single layer in a large roasting pan to avoid overcrowding. Begin with the harder vegetables and season them generously otherwise they'll be quite bland. Add the remaining softer ones and keep the cooking time as short as possible to keep the vegetables firm.

An ideal cooking temperature is approximately 200° C because the high heat ensures a short cooking time as well as golden brown vegetables.

MICROWAVING

Cooking vegetables in a microwave oven requires little or no water which ensures that more nutrients are retained. Microwave cooking also preserves and enhances natural flavours which makes it less likely that you'll add extra salt. When preparing fresh vegetables for microwave cooking, it is important that they be cut into similar-sized pieces. They should be covered to prevent the water from evaporating.

It is important to remember that food cooks faster around the edge of the dish, so arrange the food accordingly. If you're cooking vegetables whole and unpeeled, pierce them with a fork to allow steam to escape from inside. It is best to add a few tablespoons of water to the covered dish to create steam. Most hard vegetables such as potatoes, butternut, pumpkin and gem squash need water added to them.

Whichever method of cooking vegetables you choose to use, the cooking times will generally be the same. Here are some guidelines for cooking them:

VEGETABLE COOKING TIMES

Cauliflower – 8 minutes
Baby carrots – 5 minutes
Thin green beans – 5 minutes
Baby butternut – 4-5 minutes
Whole zucchini – 4-5 minutes
Baby corn – 4 minutes
Asparagus – 3 minutes
Sliced zucchini – 3 minutes
Broccoli – 3 minutes
Snow peas – 2 minutes

CREAMED SPINACH

Creamed spinach makes an excellent accompaniment to any main course. Quick cooking and high heat ensure that the beautiful green colour is retained.

1.4 kg (3 lbs)	baby spinach
45ml (3 T)	unsalted butter
175ml (¾ cup)	onion
15ml (1 T)	minced garlic
125ml (½ cup)	thick cream
125ml (½ cup)	Parmesan, freshly grated
pinch	ground nutmeg
	coarse salt
	black pepper

PREPARATION TIME: 15 minutes
COOKING TIME: 20 minutes

Wash spinach well. Place in a large pot on high heat. Toss with tongs for a few minutes to wilt. Remove from the heat, place in a colander and squeeze out as much liquid as possible. When cool, chop coarsely.

Meanwhile, melt the butter in a small pot. Chop the onion finely, then sauté with the garlic until softened. Add the cream, freshly grated Parmesan, nutmeg, salt and pepper.

Continue cooking for a few minutes until reduced. Add spinach to cream mixture and mix well. Cook until thick and creamy and most of the cream has been absorbed.

CHEF'S TIP: This is best made only a short while before serving to allow for maximum flavour.

Serves 6

EGGPLANT PARMIGIANA

My daughters love this layered eggplant dish, so I make lots of it to freeze for whenever they want some.

3 long	eggplant
	olive oil
375ml (1½ cups)	tomato basil sauce (See Pastas section, page 28)
10ml (2 t)	dry oregano
30ml (2 T)	fresh basil, shredded
300g (10 oz)	mozzarella, sliced thickly
	coarse salt
	black pepper
	Parmesan, freshly grated

PREPARATION TIME: 20 minutes
COOKING TIME: 20 minutes

Slice the eggplant lengthwise (1cm slices) with skin on and sprinkle with salt. Leave to drain for 15 minutes, then wash off the salt and dry well on paper towel.

Preheat the oven to 180° C.

Bake the eggplant drizzled with a little olive oil for about 10 minutes each side or until they are browned and cooked through. Set aside.

Spray a medium rectangular ovenproof dish.

Spread a little tomato sauce on the bottom of the dish, sprinkle with oregano and basil, top with a layer of eggplant and then a few slices of mozzarella. Repeat the layers, ending with mozzarella and a little Parmesan. Bake uncovered for about 20 minutes or until bubbling.

CHEF'S TIP: This is not a traditional melanzane, as a true Italian would dip the eggplant in flour and fry the slices in a little oil. As we are so health-conscious these days, I prefer to bake them on a baking tray in a 180° C oven. They still have some flavour and are far less oily. This dish freezes well unbaked. Defrost before reheating.

Serves 4-5

Eggplant Parmigiana

GRILLED VEGETABLES

This is a simple but effective way of serving vegetables. They look fabulous with their stripes from the grilling pan and they are loaded with flavour from the dressing. Be sure to undercook them slightly to keep them firm and crisp. This will be a winner with your guests.

80ml (⅓ cup)	olive oil
45ml (3 T)	balsamic vinegar
15ml (1 T)	fresh Italian parsley
15ml (1 T)	fresh basil
15ml (1 T)	fresh rosemary
5	zucchini
1	eggplant
2	red peppers
200g (7 oz)	thin asparagus
	coarse salt
	black pepper

PREPARATION TIME: 15 minutes
COOKING TIME: 15 minutes

Heat a grilling pan over medium-high heat or prepare the barbecue (medium-high heat).

Chop herbs and whisk together with the olive oil and balsamic vinegar. Season to taste with salt and pepper.

Slice zucchini and eggplant into long flat slices. Deseed the red peppers and cut them into quarters.

Working in batches, brush the vegetables with the herb dressing and grill them until tender and lightly charred all over: about 8 to 10 minutes for the peppers; 7 minutes for the zucchini and eggplant, 3 minutes for the asparagus. Set aside in rows for serving on a platter. Keep warm until ready to serve.

CHEF'S TIP: The grilled vegetables must only be prepared two hours before serving.

Serves 4-6

STIR-FRY VEGETABLES

A stir-fry is the best way to use up all the bits and pieces that are leftover in the fridge. Whatever you have on hand will work well. The trick to a stir-fry is to always add cabbage, bean sprouts and soya sauce last as this draws out the liquid in the vegetables.

1	onion
45ml (3 T)	olive oil
125g (4 oz)	mushrooms
2	carrots
4	zucchini
1	head broccoli
1	red pepper
1	yellow pepper
½	bok choy*
2	spring onions
75ml (5 T)	soya sauce
15ml (1 T)	sugar
	coarse salt
	black pepper

PREPARATION TIME: 15 minutes
COOKING TIME: 10 minutes

Slice onion thinly. Heat 15ml (1 T) of the oil in a wok until very hot. Sauté until golden. Then slice the mushrooms, zucchini and spring onion, and cut all remaining vegetables into thin strips, except broccoli which should be broken into small florets. Add all vegetables (except bok choy and spring onion) to onions and stir-fry until everything is just cooked, then add the bok choy and spring onion.

Pour in the soya sauce, sugar and seasonings and bring to a boil. Stir-fry everything together quickly. Serve immediately.

*Bok choy is Chinese cabbage and is available at Chinese stores throughout the year, but only in certain supermarkets during the winter months.

CHEF'S TIP: Always begin a stir-fry with the harder vegetables, ending with the ones that take the least amount of time to cook. The higher the heat, the quicker the vegetables cook and therefore will retain their colour and texture. It is important to use a wok because of its shape and size. It allows for exceptionally high heat and large quantities of vegetables.

Serves 4

Grilled Vegetables

ROAST VEGETABLES

Beautifully golden brown roasted vegetables, which are crisp on the outside and perfectly cooked inside, are one of our all time favourites. I make them this way all the time.

6	baby potatoes
45ml (3 T)	olive oil
2	sprigs each fresh rosemary, oregano, thyme
350g (12 oz)	peeled baby carrots
350g (12 oz)	zucchini
500g (1 lb)	butternut
300g (10 oz)	yellow patty pans
250g (8 oz)	mushrooms, whole
1	red onion
135g (4.7 oz)	baby corn
	Herbamare
	coarse salt
	black pepper

PREPARATION TIME: 20 minutes
COOKING TIME: 45-50 minutes

Preheat oven to 220° C

Halve the potatoes but leave the skin on. Place them in a large roasting pan. Drizzle with olive oil, season very well with Herbamare, coarse salt and black pepper. Sprinkle with fresh herbs. Roast near bottom of the oven for about 25 minutes. Then cut the zucchini, butternut and red onion into chunks, quarter the patty pans and cut the corn into two. Add remaining vegetables to roasting pan.

Drizzle with a little more olive oil, season generously again and shake the pan. Do not overcrowd the roasting pan. Continue roasting until just cooked through and softened. Total cooking time should be about 45-50 minutes.

CHEF'S TIP: The biggest problem with roasting vegetables is overcrowding them in the roasting pan where they become mushy and they don't get colour. A very high oven with a few vegetables added all the time, ensures that they get good colour and also stay firm. I season the vegetables very generously as they are particularly bland and absorb a lot of seasoning.

Serves 4-6

RATATOUILLE

A very simple recipe for a classic French vegetable dish. Simmering over a low heat, brings out the best flavour.

1	onion
45ml (3 T)	olive oil
2	medium eggplant
250g (8 oz)	mushrooms
250g (8 oz)	zucchini
1 x 410g (14 oz)	tin whole peeled tomatoes
5ml (1 t)	dry oregano
5ml (1 t)	dry basil
5ml (1 t)	sugar
10ml (2 t)	tomato paste

PREPARATION TIME: 15 minutes
COOKING TIME: 60 minutes

Slice the onion and sauté in oil until golden. Slice eggplant with skin on. Cut the mushrooms in half and add together with eggplant to onions. Fry lightly for a few minutes or until softened and browned.

Then slice zucchini thinly, add to the vegetables and continue sautéing. Lastly add tomatoes, herbs and seasonings.

Simmer partially covered on a low heat for 1 hour or until thickened and almost dry. Adjust seasoning just before serving.

CHEF'S TIP: I add the zucchini last to keep its colour. This dish can be reheated over low heat, but is best served the day it is made.

Serves 4

Roast Vegetables

There are few things more satisfying than eating a crispy roast potato or dipping a spoon into some sticky, steamed jasmine rice. But it is equally important to know how to cook something as seemingly simple as rice.

The right cooking technique will elevate a starch dish to great heights, whether it's a complement to or the basis of a main dish.

Rice

Basic Tastic Rice

Steamed Jasmine Rice

Stir-Fried Rice

Potatoes

French Fries

Roast Potatoes

Baked Potatoes

Potato Au Gratin

Mash Potato

BASIC TASTIC RICE

Although most rice packages have recipes printed on the back, I have found that there are far simpler methods of cooking.

250ml (1 cup)	Tastic rice
680ml (2¾ cups)	cold water
5ml (1 t)	salt

PREPARATION TIME: 10 minutes
COOKING TIME: 25 minutes

Wash and rinse the rice. Place rice, water and salt in a large pot and bring to a boil with lid on. Then simmer on low heat for 20 minutes with the lid on, without stirring.

Remove from the stove, allow to steam in the pot for 5-10 minutes with the lid on. Then fluff up with a fork.

CHEF'S TIP: Half a chopped onion, sautéed in a little olive oil and chicken or vegetable stock to replace the water will transform this rice into a tasty variation.

Rice cooks to 3 times its size.

Serves 5-6

STEAMED JASMINE RICE

This perfect recipe for fluffy jasmine or basmati rice is guaranteed never to fail.

500ml (2 cups)	jasmine or basmati rice
560ml (2¼ cups)	cold water
pinch	salt

PREPARATION TIME: 10 minutes
COOKING TIME: 25 minutes

Wash rice very well (about 3-4 times). Pour water over the rice and add a little salt in a large pot. Place pot on a cold stove. Turn on heat and bring to a boil with the lid on. When water is boiling, immediately turn stove down to lowest setting and time for 15 minutes. Remove pot from stove and leave rice in pot with lid on for 8-10 minutes or until steamed and fluffy.

Serves 5-6

STIR-FRIED RICE

This tasty and colourful rice is fabulous to make when there is leftover rice. It is essential to use cold cooked rice for a stir-fry rice dish.

750ml (3 cups)	cooked jasmine rice
45ml (3 T)	oil
250ml (1 cup)	frozen petits pois
3	eggs, lightly beaten
10ml (2 t)	salt
30ml (2 T)	soya sauce
3	spring onions

PREPARATION TIME: 10 minutes
COOKING TIME: 25 minutes

Heat oil in wok and stir-fry the peas for 1 minute.

Place the beaten egg in the wok and stir continuously until almost cooked. Add the rice and move the eggs on top of it. Stir-fry until the eggs are cooked through. Make a well in the centre, add the soya sauce, salt and finely chopped spring onions and stir-fry to coat the rice. Taste for seasoning. Reheat in microwave.

TO COOK RICE: See recipe for Steamed Jasmine Rice (above).

Serves 8

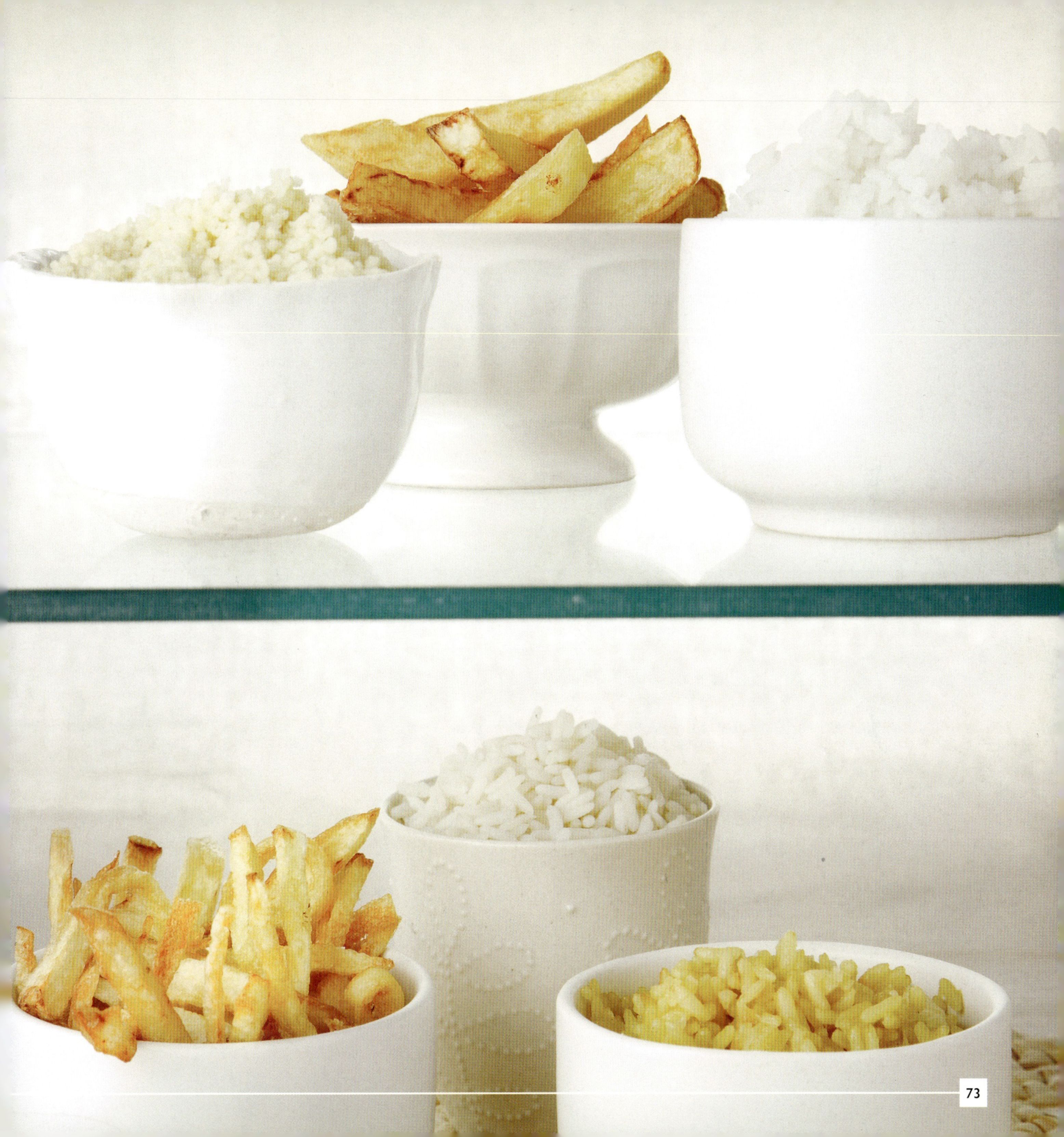

POTATOES

Whether they are baked, fried or roasted, potatoes are often thought of as the ultimate comfort food. They are an important staple food and are harvested all year round being the number one crop in the world. There are many varieties available but some are more suited to a particular method of cooking than others. Their names also vary throughout the different countries.

Baking potatoes – white and fluffy
Mediterranean potatoes – yellow and waxy
Red skinned potatoes – yellow and firm
Baby potatoes – white
Baby Mediterranean potatoes – yellow

Always keep peeled potatoes in cold water if you are not using them immediately or they will go black.

FRENCH FRIES
Allow 1 potato per person

Peel and slice potatoes into batons and leave in cold water until ready to use. Place in a pot of cold water and boil for about 5 minutes to precook. Drain well and pat dry.

Fill ⅓ of a medium pot with sunflower oil and heat until quite hot. Test with a small piece of bread.

Fry the chips until half cooked and just starting to turn brown. (This can be done much earlier in the day). Just before serving, reheat the oil and place the chips back in and fry until completely cooked.

Drain on paper towel and sprinkle with salt.

CHEF'S TIP: Always use sunflower oil when frying.

Never cover chips in the oven. Keep them warm on some paper towel in an open dish on a medium heat.

ROAST POTATOES
Peel and cut potatoes into quarters.
Parboil them following the same method as for the chips above but boil them a little longer – 10 minutes.

Fill ⅓ of a medium pot with sunflower oil and heat. Fry potatoes until just nicely browned. The oil shouldn't be too hot or else the potatoes will brown too quickly outside and not cook properly. Season with salt and pepper immediately after draining on some paper towel.

CHEF'S TIP: Don't cover rather place them on some paper towel in an open dish on a medium heat.

BAKED POTATOES
Preheat the oven to 200° C.

Prick the potatoes all over with a fork. Place directly on the middle rack and turn after ½ an hour. Bake for 1 hour. They will be hard and crispy on the outside and soft and fluffy inside. To serve, cut the potatoes open, fluff out the inside and season.

CHEF'S TIP: If you make them ahead of time, reheat them on a very hot oven as they will have gone soggy.

Roast Potatoes

POTATO AU GRATIN

In true Mediterranean style, this classic potato bake is simple and easy to prepare. Mediterranean potatoes which are yellow and waxy inside, stay firm longer when baked in a casserole dish such as this.

2	cloves garlic
30g (2 T)	butter
5	Mediterranean potatoes
625ml (2½ cups)	milk
	coarse salt
	black pepper
pinch	nutmeg
	Parmesan, freshly grated

PREPARATION TIME: 15 minutes
COOKING TIME: 45 minutes or until golden

Preheat oven to 200° C.

Rub the sides and bottom of an ovenproof casserole dish with the garlic cloves just for flavour and then discard. Rub the dish with the butter. Peel and slice the potatoes and place them in the milk in a large pot. Bring to a boil and boil for about 5 minutes to just soften them. Season the milk with salt, pepper and nutmeg to taste. (Watch that they don't catch on the bottom of the pot).

Remove the potatoes from the milk using a slotted spoon. Place them in layers in the prepared casserole dish, pour over the milk and sprinkle with Parmesan. Bake uncovered on the middle rack of the oven for about 45 minutes or until golden.

CHEF'S TIP: I like leaving the potatoes in the oven until they are crusty and well browned, so they may take a little longer to bake.

Serves 6

MASH POTATO

The secret to a really fluffy mash is to use a baking potato that mashes very well. Mashing them when warm melts the butter and ensures a really light mash.

700g (1½ lb)	baking potatoes
60ml (¼ cup)	milk
60g (4 T)	butter or margarine
	coarse salt
	black pepper

PREPARATION TIME: 10 minutes
COOKING TIME: 25 minutes

Peel and halve the potatoes and boil them in salted water until soft. When soft, drain the water, reserving about 160ml (⅔ cup). Mash the potatoes with a fork or potato masher, adding the milk, butter and seasoning. Continue mixing until fluffy and smooth, adding some of the reserved water if necessary.

CHEF'S TIP: Can be reheated in the microwave. Mash is best made by hand or with a masher, because when the potatoes are over processed in a machine, they become sticky from the gluten being released.

Serves 4

Potato Au Gratin

SAUCES

The word "sauce" is a French word that means a relish to make food more appetizing. Sauces are liquid or semi-liquid foods devised to make other foods look, smell and taste better. They enhance other dishes and can either be savoury or sweet.

Many are egg based and rely on butter or cream to thicken them and make them smooth and rich in flavour. Other sauces are enriched by reducing them over a high heat so that water content evaporates resulting in a rich-flavoured sauce. Some cannot be reheated because of their egg or butter base and need to be served immediately after making.

While there is an art to making many sauces that require great culinary skill, I have included simple and useful varieties that you will master in no time.

Whenever you are working with egg yolks, be aware that they will require refrigerating if uncooked in a sauce.

Béarnaise Sauce

Béchamel Sauce

Homemade Mayonnaise

Hollandaise Sauce

Cheese Sauce

Lemon Curd

Custard

BÉARNAISE SAUCE

The perfect accompaniment to a seared steak, this rich sauce is a classic.

½	red onion
30ml (2 T)	fresh tarragon*
pinch	salt
	black pepper
45ml (3 T)	white wine vinegar
80ml (⅓ cup)	dry white wine
2	egg yolks
90g (6 T)	unsalted butter
pinch	cayenne pepper

PREPARATION TIME: 8 minutes
COOKING TIME: 10 minutes

Chop onion finely. Heat the onion, tarragon, salt, pepper, wine vinegar and white wine in a pot and boil until reduced to 30ml (2 T). Strain into a bowl. Whisk egg yolks into the strained liquid. Place the entire mixture over a pot of hot water (which should not touch the bottom of the bowl) and whisk for one minute, adding 15g (1 T) of butter at a time, melting in between each addition and whisking gently all the time.

Remove the sauce from the hot water before it gets too thick. Lastly add a pinch of cayenne pepper and adjust the seasoning. Serve immediately or keep warm until ready to use, by keeping the bowl over warm water.

*Use either 2 T of fresh tarragon (if available) or 2 t dry tarragon. Dry tarragon is sold in SA as French Tarragon.

CHEF'S TIP: Whisk in the butter slowly otherwise the sauce might separate.

Makes 200ml (¾ cup)

BÉCHAMEL SAUCE

This basic recipe for a béchamel sauce (otherwise known as a "white sauce") can be adapted to any number of dishes and lends itself to a variety of additions.

60g (4 T)	butter or margarine
60ml (¼ cup)	flour
750ml (3 cups)	warm milk
	coarse salt
	black pepper
pinch	ground nutmeg

PREPARATION TIME: 10 minutes
COOKING TIME: 15 minutes

Melt butter in a large pot on medium heat. Add flour and stir for at least 1 minute. Slowly pour in milk, whisking as you add it. Simmer for about 15 minutes on low heat, whisking all the time to remove lumps and to cook through.

Season with salt, pepper and nutmeg to taste. Remove from stove.

CHEF'S TIP: As the sauce simmers on the stove, the texture and flavour begin to develop. A little patience produces a smooth velvety sauce.

Makes 625ml (2 ½ cups)

HOMEMADE MAYONNAISE

This mayonnaise is so easy to prepare it can be made in minutes. It is not sweet like other local varieties but is rather a classic, bland creamy mayonnaise. I use a golden yellow olive oil so as not to overpower it.

2	egg yolks
15ml (1 T)	white wine vinegar
5ml (1 t)	salt
60ml (¼ cup)	olive oil
175ml (¾ cup)	sunflower or Canola oil

PREPARATION TIME: 10 minutes

Place everything in a food processor except oil. Process. Then very slowly pour a thin stream of the olive oil and sunflower/Canola oil through the feed tube with the motor running until the mixture forms a thick mayonnaise.

Adjust seasoning.

CHEF'S TIP: Lemon juice may be substituted for the white wine vinegar.

Makes 375ml (1 ½ cups)

HOLLANDAISE SAUCE

As rich and fattening as this sauce is, there is nothing nicer to dip asparagus or fresh artichokes into once they have been steamed.

30ml (2 T)	white wine vinegar
2	egg yolks
30ml (2 T)	lemon juice
125g (8 T)	unsalted butter, cut into cubes

PREPARATION TIME: 10 minutes
COOKING TIME: 15 minutes

Whisk the egg yolks with the white wine vinegar and lemon juice. Over a double boiler*(on low heat) slowly whisk in the cut up butter, one tablespoon at a time. The water must not touch the bottom of the pot. Season with salt and a little pepper when thickened.

If not serving immediately, leave in the pot over the warm water to avoid separating.

*A double boiler is two fitted pots. The larger pot is partially filled with water brought to a simmer or boil. The inner pot uses this indirect heat to melt the sauce.

CHEF'S TIP: Sauce must be kept warm over warm water. Whisk in an extra whisked egg to the mixture, should the hollandaise separate. This sauce must be made the day it is served.

Makes 250ml (1 cup)

CHEESE SAUCE

This sauce has all the properties of a basic béchamel sauce but with cheese added. Perfect for pouring over cauliflower and baking in the oven until bubbling.

60g (4 T)	butter or margarine
60ml (¼ cup)	flour
750ml (3 cups)	milk
375ml (1½ cups)	cheddar cheese
	coarse salt
	black pepper
pinch	nutmeg

PREPARATION TIME: 20 minutes
COOKING TIME: 15 minutes

Melt butter in a large pot on medium heat. Add flour and stir for at least 1 minute. Slowly pour in milk, whisking as you add it. Simmer on low heat for about 15 minutes whisking all the time to remove any lumps and cook through until creamy.

Remove from stove and stir in grated cheddar cheese. Season with salt, pepper and nutmeg to taste.

CHEF'S TIP: This sauce freezes very well, but may need whisking after defrosting and reheating to remove any lumps.

Makes 500ml (2 cups)

LEMON CURD

This is a creamy delicious recipe which is a great base into which one could add some whipped cream or marble into some vanilla ice cream.

2	lemons – rind and juice
2	whole eggs
3	egg yolks
30ml (2 T)	milk
125ml (½ cup)	sugar
pinch	salt
90g (6 T)	unsalted butter, melted

PREPARATION TIME: 10 minutes
COOKING TIME: 20 minutes

Grate the rind of the lemons and then squeeze juice to make about 1 cup lemon juice.

Beat the whole eggs, yolks, milk, sugar, pinch of salt and butter well in a bowl with a small beater. Place the lemon rind and juice in a double boiler, add the egg yolk mixture and heat, whisking all the time over medium heat until thickened and mixture coats a spoon. This should take about 20 minutes. Cool and then refrigerate.

CHEF'S TIP: Fold some whipped cream into the curd to spread over a tart base. The curd can be refrigerated for up to 3 days.

A double boiler is two fitted pots. The larger pot is partially filled with water brought to a simmer or boil. The inner pot uses this indirect heat to melt the sauce.

Makes 500ml (2 cups)

CUSTARD

Smooth creamy custard, this one will not have the synthetic yellow colouring of the powdered variety. It will also require covering with some wax paper to prevent a skin forming on top.

4	egg yolks
5ml (1 t)	vanilla essence
250ml (1 cup)	milk
60ml (¼ cup)	sugar

PREPARATION TIME: 25 minutes
COOKING TIME: 20 minutes

Beat egg yolks and the vanilla until creamy and set aside.

Heat the milk and sugar in a separate pot until sugar is dissolved.

Slowly whisk a little milk into the egg yolks, then add remaining milk. Place over a double boiler and whisk constantly for about 20 minutes until mixture coats back of a spoon.

Remove from the heat. Cover with some wax paper as a skin will form on top and cool. Serve warm or cold.

CHEF'S TIP: For a richer custard, substitute ½ milk with cream.

Makes 375ml (1½ cups)

Lemon Curd and Custard

DESSERTS

There is no nicer ending to a meal than a sweet dessert whether it is rich and creamy or ripe, luscious fruit. It arouses the senses and lingers on the palate.

I always end a meal with something a little sweet, as simple as it might be, so that my guests leave the dinner table feeling sated, relaxed and happy.

Quick And Easy English Trifle

Basic Vanilla Ice Cream

Baked Apples

Fruit Salad

QUICK AND EASY ENGLISH TRIFLE

This dessert with its glorious colours in layers always reminds me of England.

125g (4 oz)	packet finger biscuits
	sherry or orange juice for dipping
1ℓ (4 cups)	instant custard
1 x 825g (1.8 lb)	tin sliced peaches, drained
1	box greengage jelly (half set)
1	box strawberry jelly (half set)
250ml (1 cup)	cream – whip until stiff
3-4	chocolate flake bars
3	peppermint crisp bars

PREPARATION TIME: 20 minutes

Dip finger biscuits into the sherry or orange juice. Place in bottom of a glass dish. Spread custard over biscuits. Spoon some peach slices over custard.

Spread one of the jellies over peach slices. Spread some whipped cream over jelly. Sprinkle with flake and /or peppermint crisp.

Repeat layers until bowl is filled, ending with whipped cream. Decorate with fresh strawberries. Set in fridge until ready to use.

CHEF'S TIP: This dessert can be made a day ahead but not with fruit which will go soggy and lose colour. Keep refrigerated until ready to serve. Fresh fruit such as mangoes and strawberries make a great substitute for the tinned variety.

Serves 8-10

BASIC VANILLA ICE CREAM

This makes a fabulously rich, creamy ice cream that does not need an ice cream machine. The trick is to beat the egg yolks and sugar so well that they are tripled in volume.

375ml (1½ cups)	cream (or non-dairy creamer)
4	eggs
160ml (⅔ cup)	castor sugar
5ml (1 t)	vanilla essence

PREPARATION TIME: 20 minutes

Using a Mix master, beat the cream until stiff. Set aside.

Separate eggs. Using the Mix master's wire whisk, beat yolks with half the castor sugar and vanilla essence until very thick and creamy. Set aside.

With a clean and dry whisk, in another bowl, whisk the whites until stiff and then add remaining castor sugar.

Fold cream and yolks together. Then fold in whites until entire mixture is mixed together Freeze until firm in a large bowl.

CHEF'S TIP: Use your imagination to add any number of variations to it such as chocolate chips, nuts, nougat etc.

Makes 2 litres

Quick And Easy English Trifle

BAKED APPLES

This delectable hot fruit dessert is quick and easy to prepare. I often make it and serve with a scoop of vanilla ice cream or some warm custard.

6	large Granny Smith apples
160ml (⅔ cup)	sticky brown sugar
90g (6 T)	unsalted butter or margarine, softened
125ml (½ cup)	raisins or dried cranberries
125ml (½ cup)	chopped pecans
125ml (½ cup)	apple juice
125ml (½ cup)	water

PREPARATION TIME: 15 minutes
COOKING TIME: 45 minutes

Preheat oven to 160° C.

Cut tops off apples (reserving them) and using an apple corer or a grapefruit knife, remove the insides of the apples to make a cavity large enough to fill, being careful not to cut the bottom of the apple.

Combine the sugar and butter together into a paste. Then mix in the raisins and nuts and stuff each apple with a large mound to fill it. Place the top back on the apple.

Spray an ovenproof dish and place apples standing up inside. Pour over the apple juice and water. Bake uncovered for about 45 minutes or until apples are soft, basting continuously with the juice.

CHEF'S TIP: These can be made ahead and reheated just before serving.

Serves 6

FRUIT SALAD

A fruit salad is the perfect simplest dessert using the best fruit in season. It is definitely the bowl and the way the fruit is cut that make the difference. Use ripe, unblemished fruit for maximum aroma and flavour. Remove from the fridge a half hour before serving.

apples	bananas
pears	sweet melon
papaya	mangoes (in season)
grapes	strawberries
kiwi	litchis (in season)
oranges	pineapple
spanspek	granadillas
peaches	naartjies or mandarins
plums	nectarines (in season)
	apricots

The secret to a great fruit salad is to cut the fruit into small cubes or into flat thin slices. Change the way the fruit is cut all the time, just to add some variety.

Use seasonal fruits and especially in summer it is very colourful with all the tropical fruits. But it is important to be aware of fruit that will discolour. Peaches, plums and even apricots turn brown quickly. Make sure that they are well covered in the bowl. Squeeze some lemon juice over bananas to avoid them discolouring.

Fruit salad is like a stir-fry, each whole fruit you add will make a huge fruit salad, so use minimal quantities unless you are making one for a large number of people.

Fruit makes its own juice, so a little goes a long way. The most important thing is to display the fruit in a beautiful glass bowl which shows it off best. I like to purée some fresh or tinned mangoes instead of adding extra juice.

CHEF'S TIP: A fruit salad should be served the day it is cut for best flavour.

Baked Apples

Chocolate Cake

BAKING

Although it's so easy to buy baked goods, baking is very rewarding and the results are so worth it.

There are many tricks to ensuring a successful end product – the most important being that non-stick baking tins and pans should be used for easy removal. The oven temperature should be exact. Baking on the middle rack of a preheated oven is another essential element of baking and using eggs and butter at room temperature and exact measurements are very important. Timed baking is essential but factors such as weather and different ingredients from all over the world will affect the result. When baking tarts, homemade pastry is infinitely better.

Baking blind is essential to ensure that the base is baked through and is not raw and soggy.

BAKING BLIND

This entails rolling out the dough with a rolling pin into a circle to fit the tin into which it will be baked. Careful lifting of the dough into the tin is important. Press into the tin and trim the edges. Prick base all over with a fork. Line the base with baking paper and use beans to weight it down to prevent the crust from dropping. Bake for at least 15 minutes on 180° C or until the pastry is half-set, then remove the paper and beans and continue baking the dough for another 10-15 minutes, until golden brown.

Buttermilk Scones

Asparagus Quiche

Classic Apple Tart

French Toast

Chocolate Cake

Crumpets

Sponge Cake

Pizza Dough

Crêpes With Cinnamon And Sugar

Basic Biscuit Dough

BUTTERMILK SCONES

They're light and buttery inside and with a spoon of strawberry jam and a blob of cream make the ultimate teatime treat.

600g (4 cups)	flour
30ml (2 T)	baking powder
pinch	salt
80ml (⅓ cup)	sugar
125g (4 oz)	unsalted butter
250ml (1 cup)	buttermilk
1	egg
125ml (½ cup)	water
	extra egg for glazing

PREPARATION TIME: 10 minutes
COOKING TIME: 15 minutes

Preheat oven to 220° C.

Process the dry ingredients in a food processor with the metal blade, then add the butter in cubes and process until mixture resembles fine breadcrumbs.

Beat the buttermilk and egg in a separate bowl and pulse into the dough to make a sticky mixture. Add the water. Pulse again and process until mixture just forms a ball. Remove from processor, place on a floured surface and pat down gently with your hand until dough is about 4cm thick. Use a cookie cutter to cut into 5cm rounds. Whisk an extra egg for brushing.

Spray a 12-cup muffin tin with non-stick cooking spray. Place one round of dough in each cup and then brush each with some beaten egg. Bake for 12-15 minutes.

Makes 12 scones

ASPARAGUS QUICHE

Use this pastry for any savoury filling. Simply change the vegetables but use the same basic recipe and you will have mastered a new recipe.

BASIC SAVOURY TART DOUGH

200g (1½ cups)	flour
30ml (2 T)	castor sugar
pinch	salt
150g (5 oz)	unsalted cold butter
1	egg yolk
5ml (1 t)	lemon juice
30ml (2 T)	iced water

ASPARAGUS FILLING

3	eggs
175ml (¾ cup)	cream
250ml (1 cup)	cream cheese
45ml (3 T)	butter, melted
500ml (2 cups)	cheddar cheese
1 x 410g (14 oz)	tin asparagus cuts, drained
	coarse salt
	black pepper
	Italian parsley, chopped

PREPARATION TIME: 40 minutes
COOKING TIME: 50 minutes

Preheat oven to 180° C.

Spray 26cm loose bottom tart tin or quiche dish with non stick cooking spray.

Process the dry ingredients in a food processor using the metal blade. Cut the butter into pieces and pulse in with dry ingredients. Process until mixture resembles breadcrumbs. Add the egg yolk, sprinkle the iced water and lemon juice over the mixture. Process again until mixture just forms a ball.

Remove the dough from processor, shape into a flat round covering with plastic wrap. Refrigerate for a least 30 minutes until firm.

Bake blind (see page 91). Set aside.

ASPARAGUS FILLING
Preheat oven to 180° C.

Beat eggs with cream. Add cream cheese and whisk to break up lumps. Add cooled melted butter, cheddar cheese, salt and pepper. Lastly stir in asparagus and parsley.

Pour into prepared pastry and bake for approximately 30 minutes or until puffed and golden.

CHEF'S TIP: The pastry can be made a few days ahead and kept covered with foil until ready to use. Fill and bake on the day of serving.

Serves 6

Asparagus Quiche

CLASSIC APPLE TART

Almost any fruit can be used to fill a fruit tart. The fruit should be firm and not mushy.

BASIC SWEET TART DOUGH

200g (1½ cups)	flour
30ml (2 T)	icing sugar
125g (4 oz)	cold unsalted butter
1	egg yolk
15ml (1 T)	ice water
5ml (1 t)	lemon juice

APPLE FILLING

6	large green apples
45ml (3 T)	melted butter
125ml (½ cup)	castor sugar
15ml (1 T)	cinnamon
125ml (½ cup)	raisins
125ml (½ cup)	chopped pecan nuts

PREPARATION TIME: 40 minutes
COOKING TIME: 50 minutes

BASIC SWEET TART DOUGH
Follow same method as asparagus quiche (page 92).

APPLE FILLING
Peel and slice the apples. Melt the butter in a large frying pan and lightly sauté the apples over medium-high heat until just softened. Toss with the castor sugar, cinnamon, raisins and nuts. Place in prepared tart dough and bake for another 30 minutes. Serve with whipped cream or vanilla ice cream.

CHEF'S TIP: The tart shell can be prebaked a day before serving and filled just before serving.

Serves 6

FRENCH TOAST

2	eggs, lightly beaten
60ml (¼ cup)	milk
	butter or margarine
4	slices bread
	golden syrup
	cinnamon sugar

PREPARATION TIME: 5 minutes
COOKING TIME: 10 minutes

Whisk the eggs and milk together. Heat a little butter or margarine in a frying pan. Dip the bread into the egg mixture and fry on both sides until golden.

Remove from the stove and put on a plate. Serve with cinnamon and sugar and/or a little syrup.

15ml (1 T) cinnamon plus 125ml (½ cup) white sugar for sprinkling

Serves 2

Classic Apple Tart

CHOCOLATE CAKE

This light as a feather chocolate cake has a base of egg whites which add volume, making it airy.

190g (1⅓ cup)	flour
60ml (4 T)	cocoa
7.5 ml (1½ t)	baking powder
5	egg yolks
5ml (1 t)	vanilla essence
125ml (½ cup)	oil
125ml (½ cup)	boiling water
250ml (1 cup)	castor sugar
5	egg whites
10ml (2 t)	baking powder

CHOCOLATE ICING

125g (4 oz)	butter
5ml (1 t)	coffee
60ml (4 T)	cocoa
500g (1 lb)	icing sugar
45-60ml (3-4 T)	boiling water or milk

PREPARATION TIME: 20 minutes
COOKING TIME: 25 minutes

Preheat oven to 180° C. Spray 2 x 22cm springform tins with non-stick cooking spray.

Sift dry ingredients and set aside.

Whisk egg yolks and vanilla essence in a Mix master for about 5 minutes. Add oil and boiling water and continue beating until well mixed. Pour in the castor sugar, beat again and lightly fold in the dry ingredients.

In a separate bowl, whisk egg whites and baking powder until very stiff. Fold into the chocolate mixture until all the egg whites are combined.

Divide mixture in half and pour evenly into each tin. Bake on middle rack for 25 minutes or until cake starts to pull away from sides of tin and a tester comes out clean.

Leave cake for 5 minutes to cool in the oven with the oven turned off. Remove from oven, place in a non-draughty area and cool well before removing from tin onto a baking rack.

CHOCOLATE ICING

Mix all ingredients together in a Mix master until rich, creamy and fluffy, adding more water or milk to make icing fluffy.

Spread icing over one half of the cake, then top with the other half and ice all over.

CHEF'S TIP: Cool cake completely before icing. This cake freezes very well with the icing.

Serves 8

CRUMPETS

Light and fluffy, these are moreish and divine when drizzled with golden syrup

2	eggs
30ml (2 T)	sugar
250ml (1 cup)	water
250ml (1 cup)	milk
330g (2¼ cups)	flour
10ml (2 t)	heaped baking powder
30ml (2 T)	syrup for serving

PREPARATION TIME: 10 minutes
COOKING TIME: 20 minutes

Whisk all ingredients except syrup together in a large bowl until smooth.

Spray a crêpe or frying pan with non-stick cooking spray. Heat on high till pan is quite warm.

Drop spoonfuls of batter onto pan and when bubbles appear and mixture is almost set, turn over for 1 minute. Set aside on a plate to cool before serving.

CHEF'S TIP: The mixture can be kept in fridge for up to a week.

Makes approx. 24

Crumpets

SPONGE CAKE

A classic buttery and moist cake, perfect either dusted with icing sugar or iced with butter icing which can be marbled.

250g (8 oz)	unsalted butter
375ml (1½ cups)	sugar
4	eggs
400g (3 cups)	flour
10ml (2 t)	baking powder
pinch	salt
250ml (1 cup)	milk

PREPARATION TIME: 15 minutes
COOKING TIME: 30-55 minutes

Preheat oven to 180° C. Spray a large chiffon tin or 2 x 24cm tins with non-stick cooking spray. Set aside.

Cream the butter and the sugar in a Mix master until light and fluffy. Add the eggs one at a time, beating well after each addition.

Sift the dry ingredients together. Alternate pouring in the milk and the dry ingredients into the creamed mixture and beat until well mixed, light and fluffy. Pour the mixture into the prepared tin.

TO MARBLE: Remove ¼ batter and blend with 15ml (1 T) cocoa and 30ml (2 T) milk. Whisk well. Swirl chocolate mixture on top of plain mixture and streak through with a knife to marble.

BAKE:
Large chiffon tin – for 50-55 minutes
2 x 24cm layer tins – for 30 minutes.

Remove from oven and cool well before removing from tin.

CHEF'S TIP: This cake freezes very well. It can be made into cookies using a muffin tin and iced with butter icing (use chocolate icing from page 96 but omit the cocoa). For non-dairy alternatives, substitute the butter with margarine and the milk with soya milk.

PIZZA DOUGH

This pizza dough is one of the easiest to make. It makes a thin crispy base and can be topped with any topping of your choice.

10ml (2 t)	sugar
5ml (1 t)	salt
400g (3 cups)	flour
1 sachet (10g)	instant yeast
250ml (1 cup)	lukewarm water
45ml (3 T)	olive oil

PREPARATION TIME: 10 minutes
COOKING TIME: 20 minutes

Stir all the dry ingredients into a large bowl.

Mix the water and olive oil together. Add to the dry ingredients and knead until a dough is formed.

Place dough on a floured board. Using the heel of your hand, knead the dough in an outward and inward movement, turning it all the time until smooth.

Rub some olive oil on the inside of a bowl, place dough inside, cover loosely with plastic wrap and allow to rise until doubled in volume – for about an hour in a warm place.

Preheat oven to 180° C.

Prepare two pizza tins with non stick spray. Roll out dough on a floured board to fit into the pizza tins.

Top with a variety of toppings and bake for about 20 minutes.

TOPPINGS: Tomato sauce, grated mozzarella, sliced fried mushrooms, olives, anchovies, oregano.

Serves 10-12

Sponge Cake

CRÊPES WITH CINNAMON AND SUGAR

This delicious easy crêpe recipe is great to make with your kids.

150g (1 cup)	flour
45ml (3 T)	sugar
125ml (½ cup) plus 30ml (2 T)	water
125ml (½ cup)	milk
3	jumbo eggs
30g (2 T)	unsalted butter
2.5ml (½ t)	salt

PREPARATION TIME: 15 minutes
COOKING TIME: 20-25 minutes

Melt butter and pour into food processor with all the other ingredients. Process mixture until smooth. Remove mixture, transfer to a bowl and leave to rest, covered for 1 hour (the batter may be made up to 1 day in advance and kept covered in the fridge).

Heat a small non-stick frying pan or crêpe pan on medium high heat. Spray with non-stick spray.

Pour batter into the pan, leave to bubble for a minute then quickly flip over for 1 minute on other side. Slide onto wax paper. Continue until all mixture is used, layering the crêpes between layers of wax paper until ready to serve. Sprinkle each crêpe with cinnamon and sugar and roll up just before serving.

CINNAMON SUGAR – 10ml (2 t) cinnamon to 60ml (¼ cup) sugar stirred together

Makes approx. 20 crêpes

BASIC BISCUIT DOUGH

This dough makes a delicious basic biscuit to which any number of extras can be added. They are light and crunchy because of the combination of two sugars.

250g (8 oz)	unsalted butter
125ml (½ cup)	icing sugar
60ml (¼ cup)	castor sugar
10ml (2 t)	vanilla essence
1	egg yolk
330g (2¼ cups)	flour

PREPARATION TIME: 30 minutes
COOKING TIME: 25 minutes

Soften the butter slightly and cream with both sugars in a Mix master with the "K" beater until light and fluffy. Add vanilla and egg yolk and beat to combine. Beat in the flour until it forms a smooth dough. Add your chosen variation.

Preheat oven to 180° C and line baking trays with a liner.

Refrigerate in plastic wrap for about 30 minutes before using. Cut into 5mm rounds and bake for approximately 10 minutes or until golden brown.

VARIATIONS:
1. Break ¼ dough off and mix with 30ml (2 T) cocoa powder. Set aside. Roll out remainder of dough into a rectangle. Roll chocolate dough into a sausage shape. Place on top of plain dough and roll up to make a spiral. Roll in plastic wrap and refrigerate.

2. Roll out the dough and spread with 2½ T strawberry jam. Roll up and refrigerate.

3. Sprinkle with crushed chocolate (Crunchies and Whispers are good), roll up and refrigerate.

4. Sprinkle with white chocolate chips, roll up and refrigerate.

CHEF'S TIP: The firmer the dough and the colder it is, the easier it is to cut into rounds for baking. It can be mixed with any number of variations. It can also be simply dropped in spoonfuls onto a baking tray and baked.

Makes about 40 biscuits.

Basic Biscuit Dough

TERMS USED IN COOKING

Often you will read a recipe and not know what the meaning of some of the cooking terms are. These should be a great help when interpreting a recipe.

Au gratin	A sauce with cheese
Baste	Spoon liquid over food while cooking to prevent drying
Beat	To add air with hand or electric mixer
Blend	Mix together 2 or more ingredients
Cream	Usually sugar and butter when they are mixed until light and fluffy
Dice	Cut into small cubes
Fold In	Used when adding whipped cream or egg whites to a mixture – using a rubber spatula to gently mix in
Grill	Place directly under top element of oven
Parboil	To precook for a short time before cooking another method
Purée	To liquidize or process in food processor until reduced to a smooth mixture
Sauté	Lightly cook in a little fat or oil until just cooked
Sear	To brown on either side on a very high heat to retain the juices inside the food
Herbamare	Organic herb seasoning salt
Seasoning Salt	Commercially available in supermarkets. Look for varieties without MSG

t	Teaspoon
T	Tablespoon
ℓ	Litres

OVEN TEMPERATURES

An approximate conversion chart.

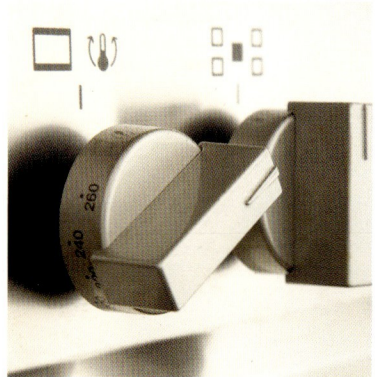

Fahrenheit	Celsius	Gas mark	Description
225° F	100° C	¼	Very cool
250° F	110° C	½	
275° F	115° C	1	Cool
300° F	120° C	2	
325° F	140° C	3	Very moderate
350° F	160° C	4	Moderate
375° F	180° C	5	Moderately hot
400° F	200° C	6	Hot
425° F	220° C	7	Hot
450° F	230° C	8	
475° F	245° C	9	Very hot

INDEX

ACKNOWLEDGMENTS

As always I would like to thank my amazing team of experts who made this book so exceptional and who made this a work of art. Without you it would not have been possible.

And of course, hugs and all my love to my darling family and friends because they are the beginning and the end.

CREDITS

AUTHOR	SHARON GLASS
PHOTOGRAPHER	ELSA YOUNG
FOOD STYLIST	ASHLEY STEWART
EDITOR	TANYA LEVITT
CONCEPT AND DESIGN	DANIELE MICHELINI
DTP	HIRT & CARTER (PTY) LTD
PROJECT MANAGER	ANTONIA VENTURINI-DE RAEDT
REPRODUCTION	HIRT & CARTER (PTY) LTD
PROOF READER	SHARON WILSON
PRINTING AND BINDING	TIEN WAH PRESS (PTE) LTD, SINGAPORE
PARTICIPATING STORES	@HOME, MR PRICE, WOOLWORTHS, GENTLY WORN, LIFE, KITCHENIQUE, BOARDMANS, LOADS OF LIVING. SPECIAL THANKS TO HOME FABRICS

ISBN NO: 978-0-620-41203-2

FIRST PUBLISHED IN 2008 BY ATV CC

PUBLISHED BY: ATV CC
www.atv.co.za

EMAIL: info@atv.co.za

WEBSITE: www.sharonsrecipes.com
www.sharonsrecipes.co.za